A REY OF HOPE

A REY OF HOPE

FEMINISM, SYMBOLISM, AND HIDDEN GEMS IN STAR WARS THE FORCE AWAKENS

VALERIE ESTELLE FRANKEL

Other Works by Valerie Estelle Frankel
Henry Potty and the Pet Rock: A Harry Potter Parody
Henry Potty and the Deathly Paper Shortage: A Harry Potter Parody
Buffy and the Heroine's Journey
From Girl to Goddess: The Heroine's Journey in Myth and Legend
Katniss the Cattail: The Unauthorized Guide to Name and Symbols
The Many Faces of Katniss Everdeen: The Heroine of The Hunger Games
Harry Potter, Still Recruiting: A Look at Harry Potter Fandom
Teaching with Harry Potter
An Unexpected Parody: The Spoof of The Hobbit Movie
Teaching with Harry Potter
Myths and Motifs in The Mortal Instruments
Winning the Game of Thrones: The Host of Characters & their Agendas
Winter is Coming: Symbols, Portents, and Hidden Meanings in A Game of Thrones
Bloodsuckers on the Bayou: The Myths, Symbols, and Tales Behind HBO's True Blood
The Girl's Guide to the Heroine's Journey
Choosing to be Insurgent or Allegiant: Symbols, Themes & Analysis of the Divergent Trilogy
Doctor Who and the Hero's Journey: The Doctor and Companions as Chosen Ones
Doctor Who: The What Where and How
Sherlock: Every Canon Reference You May Have Missed in BBC's Series
Symbols in Game of Thrones
How Game of Thrones Will End
Joss Whedon's Names
Pop Culture in the Whedonverse
Women in Game of Thrones: Power, Conformity, and Resistance
History, Homages and the Highlands: An Outlander Guide
The Catch-Up Guide to Doctor Who
Remember All Their Faces: A Deeper Look at Character, Gender and the Prison World of Orange Is The New Black
Everything I Learned in Life I Know from Joss Whedon
Empowered: The Symbolism, Feminism, & Superheroism of Wonder Woman
The Avengers Face their Dark Sides
The Comics of Joss Whedon: Critical Essays
Mythology in Game of Thrones
We're Home: Fandom, Fun, and Hidden Homages in Star Wars the Force Awakens

Copyright © 2016 Valerie Estelle Frankel
All rights reserved.

ISBN-13: 978-0692614655 (LitCrit Press)
ISBN-10: 0692614656

CONTENTS

INTRODUCTION

Most of us have seen the Original Trilogy so many times, it's taken on a life of its own in our memories. Beyond the fact that we can all quote Yoda from memory, there's also the weird distortion that happens when every single cute moment has become a T-shirt or a meme. You've probably attended a *Star Wars* wedding. *The Force Awakens* is as much a sequel to our collective memory of those films as it is to the films themselves.

In that context, a lot of *The Force Awakens* is about revisiting the big ideas of the Original Trilogy through the eyes of a new, younger set of characters, and rediscovering them. There's no way to strip away the cultural baggage that's accrued to the first three *Star Wars* films, and get at the essence of what they actually were—so instead, this film aims to connect to that collective miasma of shared ideas, while making it all new again (Anders)

While there were countless callbacks to the first film, *Star Wars: The Force Awakens* stunned many fans with its central trio – a Black Stormtrooper, a Guatemalan fighter pilot, and a woman as the Chosen One. Certainly, the industry has been heading this way, with the final *Hunger Games* film and *Mad Max: Fury Road* arriving the same year. Captain Marvel and Wonder Woman films have been scheduled, after Black Widow and Scarlet Witch took charge in *Avengers 2*. It's a world of women warriors, even on the big screen now.

The film succeeded too, making one billion dollars by day twelve – the fastest in history. It's one more step affirming that women can kick butts onscreen, that cross-racial romances are okay, that anyone can be a Jedi, or at least, use a lightsaber.

This book uses a close viewing of the film along with its prequel books, tie-in comics, guides, and so forth to discover what *Star Wars* has created in all its nuances. How does Rey

9

bring us a new kind of storytelling, and how close is her arc to the traditional heroine's mythic journey? Is Finn on the hero's journey or something else? Why is Rey being called a Mary Sue? With deep insight, it reads deeper symbolism into jungles and flaming swords, and above all, the seeing and masks so vital to the film.

Another issue to explore is diversity as women and people of color invade the galaxy smoothly -- as if they've always been standing there reading displays or taking on the Death Stars in tiny fighters. Certainly, Star Wars is trying to include modern fans of all races and genders, welcoming them to become Rebels, aliens, or even Stormtroopers. Yet in their rewrite of history and often unusual gender roles, there's a great deal of subversion taking place.

SYMBOLISM

FANDOM

Subtly, there's a heavy current of fandom in the new film. Kylo Ren is devoted to Darth Vader – beyond collecting his helmet and lightsaber, he dresses like him down to the helmet and devotes his life to Vader's goals. He vows to Vader's skull:

> Forgive me. I feel it again... the call from light. Supreme Leader senses it. Show me again the power of the darkness, and I'll let nothing stand in our way. Show me, grandfather, and I will finish what you started.

His actor Adam Driver adds that Kylo Ren is truly obsessed:

> [Kylo Ren] feels that he was actually onto something, even though in Vader's final moments where he kind of relents. That even could be interpreted as just a moment. Not to taint an entire life, or career, of doing good work. For [Kylo Ren] it's just a moment. (Woerner, "Adam Driver").

Ren mostly values "The commitment. Also, the ambition, and the loyalty. The self-sacrifice in him. They're all huge, epic things to live up to" (Woerner, "Adam Driver").

Rey, Finn, and Poe are likewise all fans of the first trilogy heroes. Poe, the child of Rebel parents, knows all the stories. "Poe Dameron grew up hearing tales of heroic pilots and their trusty astromechs, and as such, has always fostered a deep respect for his droid companions" (Hidalgo 11). In *Before the Awakening,* a stunned Poe meets General Leia Organa and she sends him on a mission. She smirks, "You should see your expression" (176). When she compares him

11

to Luke, he's "surprised and flattered at once" (178). Poe also thinks to himself in *Before the Awakening*, that he is

> ...one of the hundreds of millions – if not billions—of sentients who had been conceived in response to the Empire's fall. Poe wondered sometimes how many beings had chosen not to have children while Palpatine lived, how many had thought bringing a child into the Emperor's galaxy would be not a blessing, but a curse. (154)

Thus he owes his life to the Rebels' better world, while Rey may be the child of Luke or Leia. She too is a fangirl, struck with devotion to Han and Chewie.

> Rey: This is the Millennium Falcon? You're Han Solo? (grinning)
> Han: I used to be.
> Finn: Han Solo the rebellion general? (surprised and impressed)
> Rey: No, the smuggler
> Finn: Wasn't he a war hero?
> Rey: This is the ship that made the Kessel Run in fourteen parsecs?
> Han Solo: TWELVE! (mumbles in irritation) Fourteen...

To her wonder, he later tells her, "It's true. All of it. The Dark Side, the Jedi. They're real." Back home, she has a dead pilot's helmet and has made herself a Rebel X-wing pilot doll, crafting and collecting the way many fans do themselves. She also dresses like her idols Luke and Han, finally devoting her entire arc in the film to finding Luke Skywalker.

Even the elderly Lor San Tekka worships the Force and Jedi ideals. He's a collector of much obscure information about the Jedi – certainly something the watching fans can understand (Hidalgo 14). The *Star Wars Database* says:

> A legendary traveler and explorer, Lor San Tekka is a longtime ally of the New Republic and the Resistance. After the Battle of Endor, San Tekka helped Luke Skywalker recover secret Jedi lore that the Empire had tried to erase, and Leia Organa hopes the old scout can now help find her

brother. Following decades of adventure, San Tekka retired to live simply on Jakku, where he follows the dictates of the once-forbidden Church of the Force.

These many *Star Wars* fans filling the universe emphasize how the film's stars reflect the audience, all sharing in the joy of the franchise.

TUANUL VILLAGE

"Lor San Tekka lives in a sacred village near the Kelvin Ravine. The villagers choose to live in the wilderness so they can focus on their religion" (*Ultimate Sticker Collection* 5). This is a place of rural life and peaceful contemplation. At the Sacred Villages, "The people who live there want as little as possible from outsiders – not even goods from the outside world" (Fry, *Rey's Survival Guide*). They live simply, content with what they possess.

The Tuanul villagers worship the Force, though they cannot wield it. They enjoy a pacifist freedom to practice their faith under the New Republic: "In the time of the Empire, with the Sith secretly in command of the galaxy, any displays of worship or belief in the supernatural were against Imperial law" (Hidalgo 15). In this new world, they are unfettered at last. However, Stormtroopers invade, savagely burning the town and killing the pure innocents there.

BLOODY HANDPRINT

While Stormtroopers have been seen as a featureless unit, not much different form the lifeless, brainless battle droids of the first trilogy, *The Force Awakens* tries something different. Finn, the Stormtrooper from the earliest scene, is differentiated by his brethren because he stops to help a fallen comrade, FN-2003. That man marks Finn with his bloody handprint, one that remains on Finn's helmet through the scene. Obviously, this mark aids in distinguishing the character and showing him as more than featureless Stormtrooper. But more, it emphasizes how Finn is stained with blood on his first, violent mission. On the ship, he removes his helmet, trying to separate himself from the mark.

The Stormtroopers wear featureless, masking white as they did in the previous film – a subversion of the white – good/black – bad color scheme of myth. This also sets them apart from their masters Darth Vader and Kylo Ren. There's another nuance as it paints them as cannon fodder, a helpless sacrifice in every scene: "It is the color most associated with sacredness: sacrificial animals are often white" (Bruce-Mitford 106). Finn, of course, breaks this pattern and chooses a new path for himself.

JAKKU

The desert is a place of withdrawal from society, a quiet wildness where one can hear God or listen to the quiet voices within. It's a place of death and stillness, as many dead starships in the desert resemble skeletons. When someone is wounded at the depth of their soul, "She has first to reach the zero point, and then in complete loneliness find her own spiritual experience," journeying into the wilderness (Von Franz 98-99). Here there are no distractions or illusions, no orders to give or take, nothing but endless sand. This lifeless, stark place reflects a journey into that part of the psyche with "no impact of collective human activities" though it reflects the vast world underneath.

The desert is a negative landscape—almost nothing abides here, only miniscule plants and animals absorbing each drop of moisture, in contrast with life-filling grain fields. Many Bible heroes, such as Abraham, Jacob, Moses, Elijah, and Jesus, venture into the desert to speak with God and find enlightenment. It is "the most propitious place for divine revelation" (Cirlot 79).

The series has gotten back to the "grubbiness" of the originals ("dirty transporters, second-hand rockets, broken machinery") rather than the CGI cleanliness of Episodes I-III and its streamlined droids. This time real locations and miniature models were used when possible to mimic the seventies look. The desert filled with broken ships emphasizes this link.

FINN

Finn lands there and is separated from both the orders of the First Fleet and the friendly pull of the hotshot pilot. He sees the TIE fighter sinking into the earth and believes his rescuer, Poe Dameron, his perished. In homage, he takes the man's jacket, soon using it as a tool. "He finds Poe's jacket. he puts it on to hide his Stormtrooper uniform," explains the *Ultimate Sticker Collection* (21).

As he crosses the desert, he faces himself, alone at last, and sheds the Stormtrooper armor piece by piece to leave himself in featureless, empty black. Among knights and western heraldry, "black is associated with sin, penitence, the withdrawal of the recluse, the hidden, rebirth in seclusion, and sorrow" (Cirlot 171). He is shedding his old warrior identity for a new one.

Black symbolizes death, followed by rebirth. It is the darkness of the grave or new soil, waiting to sprout. It can also symbolize the underground world of spirit and growth. Most of all, of course, it's a total inversion of his whitewashed Stormtrooper side. Before, he spent some time in sanitation detail "doing the Empire's dirty work" on multiple levels. But now, he's his own person.

He finally wears the brown pilot's jacket, affirming himself as a rebel and everyman. By wearing Poe's jacket, he takes on the other man's job and responsibilities The humblest orders of monks wear brown, suggesting modesty and humility along with a renunciation of the material world. They are tied instead to preserving the earth, at one with nature. A leather jacket also suggests a cowboy/Indiana Jones scruffy action hero. When Rey meets Finn, the jacket alerts her and BB-8 to the fact that Finn has adopted Poe's mission. "Keep it, it suits you. You're a good man, Finn," Poe says later, referring to his fit with the Resistance as well as the coat.

Finn's name comes (ironically) from Fionn, "white" or "fair." He is the least fair-haired character around, and he discards his white Stormtrooper armor on getting his new name. Of course, this is a play on his previous name, FN-2187 (itself named for the number of Leia's holding cell). This lack of a real name suggests hidden origins – perhaps a descent from Lando Calrissian or Mace Windu (he does wield a lightsaber after all). His name, like Finnick Odair of *The Hunger Games,* evokes the Irish culture hero Finn McCool/ Fionn mac Cumhaill who leads a warband, travels to fairyland, receives a gift of divine wisdom, and otherwise performs heroic deeds, as this Finn presumably will.

REY

The name Rey, "king," is an odd choice for the protagonist. Her single-syllable first name and lack of last name, like Finn's, suggest a childhood nickname standing for something longer, which will be later revealed to the audience. Abrams, when asked, notes, "I will only say that it is completely intentional that their last names aren't public record" ("Returning Cinema's Greatest" 86).

Her name also evokes the image of a beam of light, though sunlight is yet another male symbol. Of course, "king," like "skywalker," suggests power and the heavens. Her masculine side indeed comes forth as her white tunic and desert origin evoke Luke far more than Leia. Her mask in her first appearance conceals her gender, and the dresslike shape of the tunic doesn't do much to change this. Unlike Leia and especially Padmé, famous for costume changes, Rey wears the same outfit almost for the whole movie. Her male partners actually change clothes more.

Her preferred weapon is a long pole, another male icon. Among the Tarot symbols, as well as ancient myth, the staff primarily signifies leadership as the king's scepter. Of course, hers is also a humble weapon. "Swords belonged to men in pagan Europe when most other things—fields, houses, furniture, utensils—belonged to women" (Walker 31). Thus they were a symbol of their nomadic owners – Rey too has a fighting pole but no permanent home, furniture, or garden, curling up instead in a crushed AT-AT, another symbol of masculine force. She flies the Millennium Falcon, a male space of cannons and lightspeed, and then receives a talisman of Luke's old lightsaber, a distinctly masculine symbol. Swords were given to heroes as a sacred trust, an image repeated in this case. "Often the breaking or loss of the sword signaled the loss of royal authority or of heroic mana, and the hero's consequent death" (Walker 31).

Does Rey receive nothing of the feminine?

CIRCLES

"The universe begins with roundness; so say the myths," Walker says. "The great circle, the cosmic egg, the bubble, the spiral, the moon, the zero, the wheel of time, the infinite womb; such are the symbols that try to express a human sense of the wholeness of things" (2). All these symbolize the woman in her sacred circle of the home.

Thus a more feminine weapon for the heroine would be a chakram like Xena's…or even a chakram lightsaber! Buffy on her show finally wins the scythe, a weapon emphasizing her wisdom over life and death. Wonder Woman has the Lasso of Truth. When women eschew these circles and use masculine weapons, it suggests power, but also a distancing from their feminine sides.

Rey does receive one round feminine token, though it's not a weapon. BB-8 is a pair of spheres, exuding roundness. He's childlike in size as well as his droid actions, as he shows emotion much more readily and poignantly than R2-D2. His name suggests the word "baby." Many heroines, even more than heroes, receive a magical pet or doll to care for that teaches them mothering skills. "From caring for animals, loving, and being loved, Cinderella learns she has value. She discovers herself, while the stepsisters only polish their exteriors" (Frankel *From Girl to Goddess* 37). "I named him BB-8 because it was almost onomatopoeia" Abrams says, referencing his sounds, but his baby talk only helps with the connection (Breznican "The Force Awakens" 84).

SHIPS

Ships certainly represent their owners: Amidala's ship of the prequels gleams, while the Sith Infiltrator has a cloaking device. The TIE fighter in Stormtrooper colors appears to have a malevolent red eye. A "Star Destroyer" is named for what it is. By contrast, an X-wing is small but plucky and flexible, known for speed and maneuverability, nose proudly forward. It emphasizes individual will and the power for one man to change the galaxy.

In the new film, the Millennium Falcon is still clever and adaptable, but scruffier than ever. On it, Rey proves her inventiveness and also discovers the life of a smuggler. As a symbol, the actual Millennium offers new beginnings of course. Meanwhile, the falcon is a masculine image that represents striving for great heights. It has swiftness and keen sight with great skill at the hunt (Mounet Lipp). Most of all it symbolizes freedom of the spirit "with its strength and high flight" (Bruce-Mitford 64). This bird avidly pursues its goals and never rests until they're achieved, certainly a reasonable summation of Han Solo. As Rey inherits his pilot's role on the ship, she's also given a dose of these qualities.

By contrast, Ren's shuttle resembles the classic vertical winged shuttles but in menacing black. The straight lines of Imperial shuttles with folding wings are in fact not very birdlike, but more mechanical and unnatural. Worse, his Finalizer, with its menacing name, is larger than a star destroyer, emphasizing his grandiosity and also insecurity, long before Starkiller Base is seen.

Poe's black X-wing with orange paint emphasizes his Resistance allegiance and his showoff nature. Black is the inverse of the Stormtroopers and also the color of a thief in the night, another contradiction between the stealth paint and bright orange: "Though often overlooked by sensors, the colors certainly stand out to the organic eye" (Hidalgo 13).

TAKODANA

Rey is entranced by the forest planet Takodana. "I never knew there was so much green in the galaxy," she says. With her barren, empty past, her first planet with Han and Chewie is a place of growing life and total promise. There, she's ushered to Maz Kanata's castle, the stronghold of feminine power, complete with a statue of its benefactress in front, like a clay fertility idol. It's a sanctuary, hidden and guarded: "War has not come to Takodana, as it has remained neutral throughout its long history" (Hidalgo 9). This is a former pirate stronghold, a haven for aliens of all sort who are fleeing trouble or seeking protection. It also echoes the Mos Eisley cantina, but more peaceably, suggesting its benevolent owner.

Maz Kanata, the diminutive alien played by *12 Years a Slave* Oscar-winner Lupita Nyong'o, is the first of her species seen on the show, a solitary racial outsider about a millennia old who nonetheless has built a community, much like Yoda in the prequels. Han Solo hesitantly calls the wisewoman who rules there an "acquired taste," and indeed, as she flirts in Chewie's direction and suggests control over the world by her wisdom of it, she's a powerful figure, a reimagined Yoda in perfect balance with nature.

BLUE LIGHTSABER IN THE BASEMENT

While the upper floors of a house or castle like Maz Kanata's represent the mind, basements suggest the unconscious, the world of instinct (Cirlot 153). With BB-8 (her innocence) beside her, Rey hears her own childish shrieks coming from the basement, metaphorically the place where old feelings are buried. There she sees herself facing Kylo Ren as a child.

He and his knights slaughtered the young Jedi trainees. She also sees herself in the future (presumably), chased by Ren through the snow. He is her past and future, the adversary she must face as Luke once faced Vader. There, she discovers Luke Skywalker's lightsaber in a wooden box. A closed box is a mystery waiting to be revealed. The lightsaber of course returns from the first film, emphasizing how Rey is being offered the legacy of young innocent Luke discovering the Force. This is a pathway to enlightenment and peace. "As the color of the sky and water, blue symbolizes calm, reflection, and the intellect. It is also the infinite, and the void from which all life develops" (Bruce-Mitford 107). In *A New Hope*, Luke was supposed to fly with Blue Squadron, changed to Red Squadron when the blue markings on the fighters proved difficult to film against blue screens.

On touching it, she also has flashbacks of Luke and Vader battling in Cloud City and Luke with R2-D2, so much like her own droid. These flashbacks, together with the talisman, the lightsaber, reveal her lost past as well as spiritual heritage. She is no longer ordinary but a chosen one with a mission. This reflects the journey to adolescence with its new responsibilities and powers. As Joseph Campbell describes it in his lectures on the hero's journey:

> What's running the show is what's coming from way down below. The period when one begins to realize that one isn't running the show is called adolescence, when a whole new system of requirements begins announcing itself from the body. The adolescent hasn't the slightest idea how to handle all this, and cannot but wonder what it is that's pushing him—or even more mysteriously, pushing her. (Campbell and Moyers 142)

"Such people will be aware of a dead corner within them, of something unredeemed; and the restless seeking remains" (Von Franz 96). At this point, the fairytale heroine is often driven from her superficial life. She journeys into the forest and discovers the wisdom of her unconscious, the aspects of herself she has not yet developed. This Rey does.

CLOTHES

Senators of the New Republic wear robes, emphasizing their position. Kylo Ren wears a black knight's surcoat. Finn has Poe's coat as he transforms into a Resistance fighter. In *Star Wars*, clothes are definitely a statement of who one is or wishes to become.

Phasma has a black cloak lined with red. "She wears distinctive chromed armor that broadcasts her authority but also makes clear that she is a woman of action who fights alongside those under her command" (Hidalgo 28). Mostly this emphasizes she's a warrior, not a "lady." Phasma's actress, Gwendoline Christie, explains:

> "Kathleen Kennedy said to me, 'Have you ever Googled 'female heroines'? I said, 'No,' and she did it for me. If you do it, there are a lot of scantily clad women. Now women should be allowed to dress exactly however they choose, but the idea that you Google female heroines and there isn't a diverse range of examples that come up, I find it a bit depressing." (Woerner, "Women")

As she never removes her helmet, she appears dehumanized, like a gleaming chrome statue (though silver links her with feminine power and sets her above the generic white Stormtroopers). As she actress adds, her strength comes from the concealing suit and mask.

> "And the reason I love my character so much and I feel so enthusiastic about Capt. Phasma is, yes, she's cool, she looks cool, she's a villain — but more than that, we see a female character and respond to her not because of the way she looks. We respond to her because of her actions. I think we're a society that has promoted a homogenized idea of beauty in women — and in men — and I think it's really interesting, modern and necessary to have a female character that isn't about the way her body looks. It isn't about her wearing makeup. It's not about her being conventionally feminized. The idea of this enormous legacy and franchise embracing an idea like that, which of course to many of us feels logical, is actually really progressive. And long overdue." (Woerner, "Women")

On her own sand-filled adventure, Rey begins the story swathed in concealing fabric as well, signaling a similar goal. Under it all, she is dusty and sweaty with a spray-on tan, not alluring makeup ("Queen of the Desert" 74). Her outfit is designed for desert practicality, not fighting supervillains in Wonder Woman or Power Girl's skimpy bathing suits. Critic Nicole Sperling adds:

> Her outfit doesn't sexualize her, and her hair — already nicknamed the Three Knobs — is simple, realistic and messy. "All the girls are going to want their hair to look like hers," my daughter said. Fine by me. Unlike the Girl on Fire, *Hunger Games'* Katniss Everdeen, it doesn't require an entire glam squad — or the fear of impending death — to achieve it.

Her first outfit resembles Luke's, and her second, Han Solo's. For the first time, absent of Leia's gold bikini, Padmé's royal gowns or Han's condescension, the story's heroine really appears to be in a post-gender society.

> Han – or any character, for that matter – never discourages Rey. She's never told she can't do something because she's a girl, only to later prove all the boys wrong, along with delivering some cliché remark about how girls get the job done. She proves herself capable and talented, and in turn is rewarded – never mocked. (Moran)

Now granted, this can present another problem. Second wave feminism of the sixties insisted women should avoid the makeup and high heels so they could be taken seriously. Third wave in the nineties encouraged women to dress in pretty clothes to please themselves if they wished. Rey's androgyny (to the point of swathing in face-concealing cloth and goggles) suggests an undeveloped or absent feminine side in a world where she focuses on only survival. This makes her a strong role model for boys and girls but not a very feminine one.

Her counterparts help with this, however. Rey's mentor

Maz clearly dresses just as she likes with wooden beads, silver bracelets, burgundy and teal clothes, and gaily striped knitted socks. Clearly at a millennia old, she do what she pleases. While teal suggests the serenity of the ocean and jungle and burgundy, royalty, these are also somewhat modern feminine colors, suggesting a contemporary grandma in slouchy, yet dignified fabrics.

Leia wears a Resistance uniform for most of it, in the brown that suggests simplicity. She adds a magenta vest when meeting Han. Darker pink suggests a mature feminine side, yet some sensuality and approachability toward her ex-husband.

At film's end, while sending Rey on her journey, Leia dons a long navy gown. It's a formal, businesslike color with sharp lines and cuts. There's also a crown shaped cutout at the neck suggesting royalty. "Blue has also come to symbolize purity: Christians associate it with the Virgin Mary, and it is the Roman Catholic liturgical color used on her feast days" (Shepherd 344). It's a motherly color, worn often by the women of *Game of Thrones*, and thus suitable for the powerful matriarch.

Leia's hair is an updo that echoes her classic buns. Silver earrings and an elaborate ring link her with more feminine symbolism – silvery spirituality and moon magic as much as royal jewelry. As she bids Rey farewell, she's celebrating her achievements, just as she dressed formally to reward Han and Luke after their first adventure.

CRESTS

The Old Republic's crest resembles a sun, black on white. This color pattern symbolizes perfect order, with the absolute dichotomy of truth and falsehood, right and wrong.

In heraldry, the sun, most often depicted in its splendor, represents "power, glory, illumination, vitality, and the source of life on earth" (Mounet Lipp). A masculine symbol, it represents the pinnacle of spiritual development and human achievement. Of course, this is torn down by the Empire.

Within the Star Wars universe, this image is based on the Galactic Roundel popularized by the Bendu monks, who created the earliest incarnation of the Jedi Order. The Bendu believed the circle with eight spokes unified by a single core symbolized the number nine, and with it, balance in the galaxy. On earth, such a symbol could be paralleled with the Buddhist dharma wheel (Nine is the number of the Hermit, who symbolizes self-examination and refection).

Centuries later, the Republic adopted this symbol. Fittingly for an entity of government, the number nine shows willingness to seek advice, but reversed it is stubbornness and the refusal to listen to advice.

Palpatine kept the symbol of the Galactic Roundel for himself, reducing the spokes from eight to six to fashion the Imperial Crest. It's a bit more stark, but fundamentally the same. Seven is also a number of perfection, something he clearly aspired to with galactic order but fell far short of. While there is logic in emphasizing a lack of change between governments, this also appears a reference to how the Nazis appropriated the swastika (itself a sun image and equal-armed cross symbolic of balance) from older cultures (Dodgens).

Its black and white sun-shaped crest is reminiscent of the Stormtroopers of course, themselves a transformed symbol from the Old Republic's army during the Clone Wars. "The stark white armor that was once an honorable symbol of defense was transformed under the Empire into the faceless icon of an evil regime" (Hidalgo 16).

Like the Swastika, the Empire's symbol was now reviled, so the founders of the New Republic modeled their new symbol on the Rebellion's crest (Dodgens). It resembles a blue crown, set within a circle of stars that represent the galactic community. The circle is trimmed in gold, for the right of the people to govern themselves. The crown of course suggests royal right, while the phoenix, the resurrection and immortality of the government's ideals. However, as with the sun image, the peaceful blue and celestial stars (in themselves suns trimmed in masculine gold) are brought down by a sudden attack.

The Mandalorian weapons expert and graffiti artist Sabine Wren from *Star Wars: Rebels* vandalizes Imperial propaganda with her personal sigil of a starbird, a phoenix creature. The legend stated that a starbird could never die but would always renew itself in the heart of a nova (Wallace).

> The phoenix, sometimes known as the fire bird...is a universal symbol of immortality, death by fire, the sun, and resurrection. It is also a symbol of gentleness, because it lives only on dew, not harming any living creature. (Bruce-Mitford 31)

Like much of Luke's imagery, it's a Christ symbol. The Rebellion, of course, always return, no matter how many are killed by the Empire's fire. The sun, once again, suggests masculine power and striving.

By the time of *A New Hope,* the flight helmets of the Rebel X-wing pilots are adorned with a similar logo, now a bit more abstract and crownlike. In homage, the Resistance adopt the same emblem: "the starbird." The logo of the Resistance is specifically the same as the logo of the Rebel Alliance, emphasizing that the New Republic is not responsible for their behavior. In the new film, the Rebellion has indeed risen from the ashes to attempt a new uprising.

By contrast, the New Order's crest is red and black, either a bloody sun or a circle of black spikes pointing inward to stab those caught in their trap. Either way, while it adapts the sigil of the Empire, it is deadly in a new and disturbing way.

NEW ORDER

The goosestepping Nazis famously echoed World War II, in a world that had confronted evil directly. The pattern of events in *Phantom Menace* as Palpatine legally seizes power through manipulation echoes Hitler's putsch of 1933. Many of the proper names in the films were derived from French, Japanese or Hindu, all reflecting the roles these countries played in the conflict. Likewise, the black cloth uniforms with caps reflect the SS uniforms.

This time around, the name "New Order" emphasizes the connection as the Stormtroopers rise again in a second Reich, one might say. There's a German battleship gun turret Han, Finn, and Chewie climb through on the ice planet (Szostak 214). A legion of Stormtroopers give their evil leader a Nazi salute as he addresses the masses from a stage in scenes reminiscent of Hitler's famous speeches. Likewise, the uniform worn by General Hux resembles Nazi uniforms mixed with some naval influences.

Significantly, Abrams compares the First Order to Nazis who fled to South America and wanted to follow Vader's vision. "Could the First Order exist as a group that actually admired the Empire? Could the work of the Empire be seen as unfulfilled? And could Vader be a martyr?" he asks. "Could there be a need to see through what didn't get done?" (Breznican, "The First Order" 90)

HOSNIAN PRIME

It was decided that all worlds would have equal say in the shaping of government. This change resulted in the capital of galactic politics moving from Coruscant, its home for millennia, Member worlds would now host the Senate on a rotating basis. (Hidalgo 9)

Coruscant, the metropolis planet of the old order, may not be the same as Hosnian Prime, but it fills the same function. Both are at one time the capital of the Republic. Both are giant metropolises far from the nature worlds of the Rebels or the backwater desert worlds where Luke and Rey begin. When the New Order destroy Hosnian Prime, it shatters the old way of life, of stuffy senators in their disciplined robes and civilization to return the universe to the law of the jungle.

STARKILLER BASE

The snow planet, like the Stormtroopers, has been

stripped of its name and transformed into a savage weapon, shrouded into featureless white. Its frozen environment casts a wintery backdrop against the First Order's blood-chilling goals. It's been mutated to serve the murderous regime. The novelization adds:

> Spectacular and isolated, with a mean surface temperature varying from merely cold to permanently arctic, the planet had been altered: its mountains tunneled into, its glaciers hacked, and its valleys modified until it no longer resembled its original naturally eroded form. Those who had remade it had renamed it.
> Starkiller Base.

Winter reflects sterility, as in Narnia, where it's "always winter and never Christmas" until the deadly snow melts with Aslan's arrival. Ice symbolizes a rigidity, and the death of potential as water is rendered immobile. In this form, it cannot nourish crops, only hold the world in featureless white stasis. There's also a sense of universal waste – this planet's water might nourish pilots or the desert planet, but instead, is converted into a planet-sized death star.

On this planet, as on Takodana, Rey flees into the wilderness. There she finds a small amount of shelter, but as Luke must in the cave, she faces the terrible force of destruction, masked and evil.

KYLO REN

Kylo Ren wears a black surcoat with no insignia – suggesting a blackness of heart with no true cause. Among knights, "black is associated with sin, penitence, the withdrawal of the recluse, the hidden, rebirth in seclusion, and sorrow" (Cirlot 171). The leather creases of his sleeves look mummylike or reptilian. His star destroyer is The Finalizer, emphasizing his mission of destruction.

"In the West, black is the color of death, mourning, and the underworld. It also has associations with evil magic" (Bruce-Mitford 106). Kylo Ren appears a copy of Darth

27

Vader, who uses the Dark Side and wears black robes and a metallic black mask with a re-breather. This is a deliberate homage, as he's seen kneeling before a shrine containing his grandfather Vader's burned helmet, praying for guidance:

> "Forgive me. I feel it again... the call from light. The Supreme Leader senses it. Show me again, the power of the darkness, and I'll let nothing stand in our way. Show me, grandfather, and I will finish what you started."

He is caught between two identities, two families, two missions, born and raised as he was in both the goodness and the memory of villainy. In fact, his helmet also echoes Stormtrooper helmets, Jedi Master Plo Koon's mask, and Darth Revan's, stressing his ancestral heritage of evil. His actor explains:

> The costume really says a lot about him before he says anything. [Kylo Ren's] helmet is unpolished and unfinished. It's not refined. It's shiny in parts and reflects back what it sees. These are all metaphors that you can't really play, but it's good information. (Woerner, "Adam Driver")

Kylo Ren's weapon is an unstable lightsaber, reflecting his unstable self warring between dark and light. Abrams notes: "The lightsaber is something that he built himself, and it's as dangerous and as fierce and as ragged as the character" ("Returning Cinema's Greatest" 86). "It has three blades instead of one and looks more like an ancient sword" (*Ultimate Sticker Collection* 15). This combined with Ren's surcoat emphasizes his status as knight, serving the forces of darkness in the ancient conflict.

New to the world of lightsabers onscreen (though it's been seen in the Expanded Universe) it has a crossguard of two smaller blades. While this looks impressive, it's much more dangerous for the wielder, threatening to slice his hand with every use. His blade is not a dangerous "two-edged sword" but a "three-edged sword" – he is in a terribly precarious place. "The stressed crystal barely contains the power of the weapon, necessitating lateral plasma vents that becomes the crossguard quillions" (Hidalgo 26). This speaks to his inexperience and lack of skill as well as pulsating rage so much that the materials around him are cracking. His actor adds: "His lightsaber, you got the sense that it was homemade, and it could spontaneously combust at any minute. It didn't really seem like it was really reliable" (Woerner, "Adam Driver").

Obviously, Sith Lords carry red lightsabers. "Red is the color of life – of blood, fire, passion, and war" (Bruce-Mitford 106). These suggest the violence and hellfire their wielders bring to combat. It's also the color of martyrdom – and indeed, these Sith lords are sacrificed for the good of their masters, until Vader chooses to sacrifice himself.

WEIGHT OF THE PARENTS

Snoke, Kylo Ren, and Captain Phasma all tower over the protagonists: This emphasizes their influence as Finn fights off his orders from Phasma and Kylo Ren intimidates Rey as he did when she was a tiny child (in fact her childhood flashback emphasizes this dynamic).

Snoke, in particular, is over seven feet tall, or so he appears on the holoprojection. He apes many of Palpatine's mannerisms. One popular fan theory is that he's the original, even primordial parent in this dysfunctional family – if Vader was the father of the last film set, and Palpatine the grandfather (metaphorically, in terms of training and influence), decaying, scarred Snoke might actually be the Sith trainer of Palpatine himself, Darth Plagueis, introduced in *Revenge of the Sith:*

> Darth Plagueis was a dark lord of the Sith, so powerful and so wise. He could influence the midichlorians to create life. He had such a knowledge of the Dark Side, he could even keep the ones he cared about from dying.

Is he still manipulating the universe from his zombielike

body?

Ren kneels to him and to Vader's skull, both times giving them visual power over himself. "You're afraid... that you will never be as strong as Darth Vader!" Rey notes, reading his mind and discovering his deepest fear.

MASKS

Even Rey starts the film with her face shrouded. Though this is meant as protection from the sand, it certainly adds a surprise reveal. In turn, Finn rips off his mask to show his horror at the Stormtroopers' actions. This of course humanizes him. Meanwhile, Phasma the Chrome Trooper, demands he put it back on while on their ship. She herself never removes her mask, emphasizing the facelessness of all the enemies in this film. She demands Finn abandon all traces of individuality, though he stubbornly resists her.

The thugs that attack Rey to steal BB-8 keep their faces shrouded to avoid later reprisals and are bundled all in black. Attacking the Falcon later are Guavian security soldiers. They go masked in red with a black ring in the center, "giving them an even greater air of menace" (Hidalgo 53). In fact, these masks were originally envisioned for a killer Jedi (Szostak 143).

Kylo Ren maintains his own cruel mystique with his iconic mask. Here, "silver inlay radiates from the eyes as a symbol of power" (Hidalgo 24). Resisting all the emphasis on sight and eyes from Maz, his mask blocks all. He also wears it in homage to his idol, as he also worships Vader's burned helmet on a pedestal and begs it for guidance. "Darth Vader's charred and melted helmet is a silent symbol of both the Dark Side's strength and its weakness" (Hidalgo 24). His actor reveals:

> The eyes were a thing that J.J. and I talked about early. I thought what was so great about the [Darth] Vader mask was how you projected your emotions onto him, and you could see his eyes. I was kind of nervous that in being fully cloaked, you have to really rely on the power of thought,

and that it's powerful enough that it will get through being concealed. Then J.J. actually took out the eyes out of the mask, to make it a void, which I thought was really interesting... there was something about someone who decides to completely hide themselves that I felt was kind of interesting, and maybe that's hopefully worked its way into the movie. (Woerner, "Adam Driver")

It's clearly meant to intimidate, as Vader's always did, and Rey calls him on it:

Ren: You still want to kill me.
Rey: That happens when you're being hunted by a creature in a mask.

When Rey pushes him thus he removes it for the first time in the film, revealing to her surprise, a normal, even handsome young man. It does not conceal a Vader-like disfigurement or keep him alive – it only serves to conceal himself.

When Han arrives, he calls Kylo by his real name, Ben, and urges him to unmask, emphasizing that he doesn't need it to face Han but can simply be his old human self.

Han Solo: Take off that mask. You don't need it.
Kylo Ren: What do you think you'll see if I do?
Han Solo: The face of my son.

Ren does, indicating his vulnerability as well as his conflicted nature. With his pained, struggling face showing, he kills Han, who in turn touches the unmasked face, connecting with the person his son once was.

FIRE AND ICE

After Ren murders his father, the red and blue lights that surrounded them turn red as the light on his face, indicating his struggle between dark and light has ended. The wide shot of the light hitting Han and Ben is "the Force essentially making its decision" Key Jenkins says (Szostak 221). At his act against nature, Chewie sets off the explosion, turning his own grief into physical destruction. Fire rains down from the

31

sky outside and Rey and Finn escape into a world of black and red. The world is crumbling in reaction.

"As long as there's light, we got a chance," one X-wing pilot insists. Since the Starkiller weapon is draining the sun, this is literally true, but it also works on all the symbolic levels, of course. At true darkness, they are all doomed.

As Rey and Ren, parallel down to their names, fight outdoors, fire and explosions rain down, opening fiery cracks in the earth. In the snow battle, dead branches are scattered like lost hopes. This warring background reflects their personalities, his chaotic fire and her controlled ice. Their red and blue swords clash. In her soft beige, Rey blends with the snow, a force of nature. She channels calmness, coolness, icy dispassion. This gives her the strength to win. At last, only a fiery chasm's opening saves Ren. Triumphant, Rey flees with Finn and Chewie as the planet dissolves into fire, the result of Ren's grim handiwork.

LUKE'S HAND

Hands are the way we interact with the world. Thus having one amputated destroys human power and cuts one off from others. Luke, who already lost his hand, now has the same or a different prosthetic that's silver rather than skin-colored. Possibly the synthetic skin of the hand has worn off, or Luke just doesn't bother hiding it any more. These both indicate a lack of obsession with appearances and a path away from worldly vanity.

There are many myths of characters with silver hands – Nuada of the Silver Hand is given such a gift so he can be fit to be king. Perhaps in homage, Wormtail receives a similar hand after Voldemort makes him cut the first one off. Both of these characters gain agency back from the substitute. The armless maiden has her own real ones chopped off, and her prince gives her silver hands to take their place, though they do not work. These indicate a transitional stage, nebulous magical hands, before she earns the return of her real ones. Luke's story is more likely the former than the latter (though if he dies and becomes a Force ghost, he will presumably have two hands this time). Nonetheless, the magical and spiritual symbolism of silver should not be discounted.

After becoming a Jedi in his last film, Luke Skywalker has also grown a beard, bringing him closer to elderly Obi-Wan and Qui-Gon as well as emphasizing his role as the aging hermit in the wilderness.

FINDING LUKE

Seeking Luke, Ray climbs uphill, emphasizing her spiritual ascent. He lives on a green world with a stretching sea, emphasizing the next step he can offer in her spiritual enlightenment. She gives him back his lightsaber, thus connecting him to the young hero he was and can be again with Rey, his spiritual heir.

Of course, Luke's absence for the entire film is notable as it turns into a quest to find him. One of the scriptwriters, Michael Arndt, explains:

> "Early on I tried to write versions of the story where [Rey] is at home, her home is destroyed, and then she goes on the road and meets Luke. And then she goes and kicks the bad guy's ass. It just never worked and I struggled with this. This was back in 2012."
> "It just felt like every time Luke came in and entered the movie, he just took it over. Suddenly you didn't care about your main character anymore because, 'Oh f–k, Luke Skywalker's here. I want to see what he's going to do.'"
> (Keyes)

Certainly, he's a powerful enough fighter that Rey's characterization would have been quite squashed if she spent the entire film as Luke's sidekick. She and Han would have had to step back to let Luke face Kylo Ren in Luke's millionth battle with the dark side. It would have been even more a rewrite of the previous films.

> Instead, Luke is a myth of sorts, like the Force and the Jedi. We learn what he attempted to do after *Return of the Jedi,* forming a new academy to teach new Jedi just like he

did in the Star Wars Legends (Expanded Universe) books. He failed and left, believed to have gone to search out the original Jedi temple or to protect something the First Order is seeking out. We'll find out more in May 2017 with Episode VIII. (Keyes)

Thus as he deserts the galaxy and allows his friends to find him when the time was right, Luke allows them to evolve on their own, yet sets up the next stage of the quest. The map and R2-D2's guidance may even have been waiting for Rey herself. He may take the Yoda role in the next film, training Rey, telling her the deep secrets of her heritage, then allowing her to journey forward.

THEMES

- Family: Original *Star Wars* uses the family dynamic as a metaphor for the political situation and the struggle of dark and light. Luke Skywalker must accept his conflicted feelings about his father, stop his tyrannical reign and try to save him, all while reconciling feelings for his sister that are finally admitted to be more platonic than romantic.

  The new *Star Wars* continues this dynamic based heavily in metaphor: Kylo Ren can turn utterly to evil by murdering his good father as the man tries to love and redeem him. In both stories, the father-son conflict turns violent, expressed through the duties of good and evil.

  Rey is devoted enough to her family to remain, near-starving on the backwater of Jakku and constantly insist on returning there. Luke's being her father is supported by the narrative as her quest for answers and to discover the truth of herself leads her to his hideaway.

- Friendship is equally important, as Luke, Leia, and Han form a world-saving partnership, long before two of them are revealed to be related and another two fall in love. The new trilogy offers a similar trio, as Poe rescues and names Finn, then Rey and Finn save each other from evil. "We've all felt alone and powerless and most of us have been saved from that by friends who join us in a shared destiny, whether it's a personal journey or a common dream," one critic interjects (Breznican, "The Force Awakens" 83).

- Resisting authority: The heroes are not the Senate or New Republic, but the ragtag resistance fighting from the shadows with limited resources. They battle the vast and powerful Empire or New Order – both terms that suggest totalitarian power.

- Duty and larger responsibly versus the personal: Luke must choose between his training with Yoda and saving his friends as they're being tortured. He's pulled in different directions by Leia – who is all political duty – and Han Solo, who values his friends but not any cause. Padmé and Anakin retell this dynamic for a new generation. The newest series has Finn wanting only to save Rey while Han cares only for saving his son – both jeopardize the mission through their mixed agendas. Meanwhile, Rey must give up on her awaited family to train as a Jedi. *Star Wars* profoundly asks, "Can a choice be both selfish and selfless," like Luke's abandoning his mission and surrendering to Vader to redeem him (Barr 10).

- Celebrating good leadership: When General Leia is mentioned early in the movie, elderly Lor San Tekka says, "To me the general is royalty." Nonetheless, she has presumably earned her general status the hard way, as has Ackbar. Both have given up their roles in the Senate to fight the darkness they know is coming. Likewise, when Rey asks Han, "Is that possible (to fly warp speed and then suddenly stop)?" he answers, "I never ask that question until after I've done it." Courage and will are paramount.

- Struggle between Light and Darkness:

> Snoke: There has been an awakening. Have you felt it?
> Kylo Ren: Yes.
> Snoke: The dark side, and the light.

As Darth Vader's grandson (and Han and Leia's son) Kylo Ren has always been poised between these. He makes a clear choice here, as do Rey, Finn, and Poe, who are all offered the option to surrender to the dark.

✓ The weight of history and legacy: Finn, who has grown up a Stormtrooper, must shake this off. More, Rey grows up in the wreckage of past battles. The war they're caught up in rose from the aftermath of the Rebellion of the original trilogy, which in turn was a battle against Palpatine's regime built in the prequels. Legends of Luke and Han form everyone's cultural consciousness, and Kylo Ren is desperately trying to live up to another hero – Darth Vader. Snoke, the oversized primordial authority, looms above it all.

✓ Power of love: Luke's love for Ben, Leia, and Han saves the galaxy and sets him on the path of goodness, while Anakin's angry, uncontrolled love for his mother and Padmé burns down the galaxy. Nonetheless, his love for his son redeems him. Han's for his own son and Finn's for Rey guides the events this time around. In the novelization, Snoke adds:

> "Kylo Ren, I watched the Galactic Empire rise, and then fall. The gullible prattle on about the triumph of truth and justice, of individualism and free will. As if such things were solid and real instead of simple subjective judgments. The historians have it all wrong. It was neither poor strategy nor arrogance that brought down the Empire. You know too well what did."
> Ren nodded once. "Sentiment."
> "Yes. Such a simple thing. Such a foolish error of judgment. A momentary lapse in an otherwise exemplary life. Had Lord Vader not succumbed to emotion at the crucial moment—had the father killed the son—the Empire would have prevailed. And there would be no threat of Skywalker's return today."

REY'S HEROINE'S JOURNEY

Star Wars, with innocent Luke's growth into maturity, is often used to teach the hero's journey. *A New Hope* and the original trilogy cover the cycle perfectly, and the prequel has some nods to it too. With the new film, the question must be asked: what of the heroine's classic quest? Though it's less seen in the great epics of the world, in contrast with the legends of Moses, Jesus, Hercules, Odysseus, King Arthur, and others worldwide, it goes back just as far. Around the world, Sumerian Inanna, Greek Demeter and Persephone, Isis, Brynhild, Anat, Copper Woman, Pele and Hi'iaka all descend into darkness to gain their hearts' desire. Many fairytales, too, follow the pattern. In modern times, heroine's journey adventures appear in *The Hunger Games, The Wizard of Oz, Narnia, Coraline, The Mortal Instruments, Buffy, Xena, Dark Angel, Supergirl, Wonder Woman,* and many more.

> Rey grows in confidence through encouragement, and with a strong belief in herself and her abilities she is able to achieve great things. It's the quintessential hero's journey, and with how strongly *The Force Awakens* mirrors *A New Hope,* the striking similarities between Rey's and Luke's journeys aren't at all surprising. In both films their eyes are opened to a larger world and they face great challenges, which they surpass, but not without suffering loss. (Moran)

This is valid analysis, though in fact the hero's journey and the heroine's are in some ways strikingly opposite. The first great difference is the goal of the quest: The hero quests to destroy the Dark Lord, as Harry Potter, King Arthur, and Luke Skywalker do. All Luke wants to do is leave Tatooine and go on adventures. By contrast Rey is seeking her family and chooses to find them by staying home. "She lives alone and wishes she had a family to care for her" (*Ultimate Sticker Collection* 3). The quest for family is classic heroine's journey as she grows into the protector and savior – many tales see the woman journeying into fairyland to retrieve a stolen child, for instance.

> Her goal is to become the all-powerful mother. Thus, many heroines set out on missions to rescue their shattered families: Meg Murray of *A Wrinkle in Time* quests to save her father then her little brother. Coraline tries to save her parents, Meggie of *Inkheart* and Clary of *The Mortal Instruments,* their mothers. Tim Burton's Alice tries to rescue the Mad Hatter. Scores of young women in folklore rescue their lovers from fairies, demons, and ogres. Demeter forces herself into the realm of the dead to reclaim her daughter, while Isis scours the world for her husband's broken body. Katniss, of course, spends the series protecting Prim and her growing adoptive family, from Peeta to the children of Panem. (Frankel, *Many Faces of Katniss* 113-114)

Another token of both hero and heroine is the mystery origin or divine birth. King Arthur, Harry Potter, and Luke himself are all foundlings with noble ancestries. Certainly Rey's short name, like a nickname, suggests there's much more to the story. With her upscale Coruscant accent, she appears to come from the central worlds rather than the distant desert of Jakku. She's clearly a princess in exile.

The film emphasizes her connections to Luke, from desert origins to speeder to her clothes to her skill with the Force. His lightsaber flying into her hand only seems a confirmation of her parentage. In the novelization, when Ren sees this he thinks, "It is you," clearly aware of who she is. Of course, she might be simply a talented young student of Luke's or Han and Leia's child (if they've been made to forget her). The couple are each very affectionate from the start, but both accept her desire to seek her family rather than keeping her close. She seems comfortable aboard the Millennium

Falcon – too much for a newcomer, as she knows where the gunner position is, and how to fix it and also spots the modifications. Jedi training in her past would explain her familiarity with the Jedi mind trick and her lightsaber skill.

Buried in her head is an image of a watery island where Luke awaits her, suggesting that from the start she's been given this one talisman to prove her identity and mission. While in the film, Snoke's last line is "It is time to complete his training," he adds in the novelization, "It appears that he may have been right about the girl." Clearly an awesome destiny awaits her.

Following the male pattern, Rey grows up a scavenger swathed in enough fabric that she appears androgynous. Her trusty weapon is a staff – in fact, Daisy Ridley studied bojutsu to wield it correctly ("In the Shadow" 93). All this is a form of protection on the rough planet. She lives in the Goazon Badlands between Niima Outpost and the Kelvin Ravine by Carbon Ridge and the Sinking Fields, where all the names sound ominous. "I've been here my whole life, scratching out a living with the lost and broken," she notes (Fry, *Rey's Survival Guide*).

However, her great task there is the feminine role – to endure: "Thousands of scratches are a testament to her tenacity and survivor's instinct" (Hidalgo 30). She has been told to await her family's return, so she does. In the novelization's telling of her childhood flashback, Rey hears a voice say, "Stay here, I'll come back for you." She whirls, trying to find the voice through the trees. "I'll come back, sweetheart, I promise." This memory is her only talisman, with no other guidance.

> "I don't know if Rey is really about anything in the beginning of the film except for working and feeding herself," Ridley says. "Her life is pretty ... 'mundane' is the wrong word ... but it's pretty repetitive. She's literally living hand to mouth. She's solitary. She doesn't speak to people very much. She's just trying to make it work for herself." (Woerner, "Women")

Describing the AT-AT in her prequel journal, Rey notes, "I spend most of my time inside the belly." This is a womb image, of the heroine not yet born, still content to be sheltered rather than act in the world (Fry, *Rey's Survival Guide*). This is another classic heroine pattern. As Joseph Campbell commented in one of his later books:

> In *The Odyssey*, you'll see three journeys. One is that of Telemachus, the son, going in quest of his father. The second is that of the father, Odysseus, becoming reconciled and related to the female principle in the sense of male-female relationship, rather than the male mastery of the female that was at the center of *The Iliad*. And the third is of Penelope herself, whose journey is ... endurance. Out in Nantucket, you see all those cottages with the widow's walk up on the roof: *when my husband comes back from the sea.* Two journeys through space and one through time. (*Pathways to Bliss* 159)

In an early nod to the perception theme, Rey even gathers flowers as she waits "to remind myself that there's beauty everywhere if you look hard enough, even on Jakku" (Fry, *Rey's Survival Guide*).

> When she looks at an old, wrinkly women cleaning scrap for sale, then later wistfully at a ship leaving the planet, it's clear Rey is worried she'll spend her whole life wasting away on Jakku. She wants to leave, to seek adventure, even if she doesn't fully admit it to herself. (Moran)

While she has this trace of femininity, she also seeks stronger masculine weaponry: She considers buying "a blaster perhaps so she could better protect herself, instead of having to rely on her staff" in the prequel short story in *Before the Awakening* (79). The book adds, "She wasn't afraid of violence. She didn't enjoy it but she wasn't afraid of it. It was a necessary part of surviving on Jakku" (107). Toughness is valued here, rather than sentiment. "She was good enough that the word had spread in Niima to stay clear of her and what she could do with her staff" (Rucka, *Before the Awakening* 107). Traditionally, the classic Warrior Woman – Mu Lan, Atlanta, Athena, Artemis, Éowyn, Batgirl, Xena, Buffy, Katniss – fights with masculine weapons and has a male mentor and a male nemesis. Often she disguises herself as a boy or wears men's clothing or armor. Women are more likely to fight with distance weapons – bows, spears, the lasso, the whip, and the chakram in this list of warriors. Rey's staff provides a little of that separations only guardian is the unfeeling male trader Unkar Plutt who gives her a pittance for her labor. Two portions is "barely enough food to silence her stomach for a day" (Rucka, *Before the Awakening* 61). He may be the one who raised her when she first arrived, or even the slaver who bought her – in the flashback where she's abandoned, the arm in the shot resembles Plutt's. Despite the harshness of the lifestyle, she lives on faith – that one day, if she sticks it out, she will earn back her family.

> The child on the Chosen One's path leaves his or her birth family to find a better one, a "real" one. "My family doesn't appreciate me, and they're so boring. I must be adopted. I must not belong here, but somewhere more magical and special," the child thinks. (Frankel, *Buffy* 36)

As with Luke, Cinderella, and most other characters, a catalyst jolts Rey from her everyday existence. Campbell scholar Christopher Vogler explains, "The hero is presented with a problem, challenge, or adventure to undertake. Once presented with a Call to Adventure, she can no longer remain indefinitely in the comfort of the Ordinary World" (15). This is the droid BB-8, wanted by the Empire. When Rey sees scavengers carrying him off, she intervenes, and saves him. Rey tells BB-8 that the scavenger who's captured him "wants you for parts. He has no respect for anyone" and fixes his antenna as if wiping his chin. She, by contrast, respects all innocent life. BB-8's name suggests he's a baby, and as Rey protects him, this image gains strength. His mannerisms also underscore the connection. Chief of creature and droid effects Neal Scanlan says, "We always saw BB-8 as a naughty puppy or a very clever little child. They know how to be coy, how to be cute, how to sulk, how to pull at heartstrings to get what they want" ("BB-8" 63).

BB-8 represents the heroine's vulnerable innocent side, though he brings more as well: Scanlan adds: "Daisy Ridley spent a lot of time around BB-8, who is using all these tricks to transport himself on this important journey. He's on a mission, and he has to succeed" ("BB-8" 63). Metaphorically as well as literally, he offers her a sense of purpose

The ships she fixes are more child-substitutes, teaching her nurturing. As her prequel book adds, "She had found a spacecraft that had lain in the sand for years – decades even – and nursed it back to health. She had, with her hands and her smarts, taken it into the air once more. That was something to be proud of" (Rucka, *Before the Awakening* 105).

"Classified, really?" Rey asks BB-8 after he responds to her question of where he comes from. "Me too." Both are mysteries, both isolated and in need of friendship. BB-8, more importantly, brings her her quest. Saving BB-8 leads to finding Finn, being attacked, and finally escaping the planet with Finn and BB-8 on the Millennium Falcon, where Rey meets Han and Chewie.

One's companions on the quest are meant to fill in what is missing in one's personality. The male side of the self, or Animus, as Jung called it, "evokes masculine traits within her: logic, rationality, intellect. Her conscious side, aware of the world around her, grows, and she can rule and comprehend the exterior world" (Frankel, *Girl to Goddess* 22). At the most primitive level, the Animus is a force of brute strength and power (Unkar Plutt, who controls her food and gets his way with hired goons).

As the heroine matures, her Animus grows with her or is replaced by wiser ones when she's ready for his more developed stages: initiative and planning, rule of law, and wisdom. Finn, Han, and Chewie drag her into battle with

Han's impulsive plans, showing that they're at this level. Finn, too, is not yet a source of morality but expediency:

> Poe Dameron: Why are you helping me?
> Finn: Because it's the right thing to do.
> Poe Dameron: ...you need a pilot.
> Finn: I need a pilot.

Despite this, while Rey looks out for only herself, all her new friends are used to battling for a larger cause...though in Finn's case, it's the cause of a Stormtrooper. He has the military discipline she lacks, and all the others have the combat experience. Together they train her to prepare for the unknown and also protect her companions.

.Along with an upgrade in her male team, she receives one in armaments as Han offers her a blaster.

> Han Solo: You might need this.
> Rey: I can handle myself.
> Han Solo: I know. That's why I'm giving it to you.

Rey's LPA NN-14 blaster is compact for her small hands and silver. This is a feminine color in symbolism, suggesting spiritual power. It represents the Otherworld: feminine moon and water magic (Walker 522). Artemis' bow, the divine amulets of the Egyptians, and the sixth chakra, often called the "third-eye" of special perception, were all particularly feminine talismans. In medieval times, silver was a purifying element that could shield its wearer from maladies and monsters. Leia and Maz, the story's other powerful women, also have small silvery blasters.

Han's trust and partnership, offered at the same time as the weapon, help set her on her path. He mentors Rey, seeing her as a worthy successor or co-pilot for the Falcon when Chewie's injured. He even offers her a job.

> Many remember the [original Falcon battle] scene and Han's now famous response to Luke's joy and astonishment – "Don't get cocky, kid!" But when it comes to

> Rey, Han is all about encouragement. This is due in part to Han having a different relationship with Rey than Luke, more mentoring than rivalry, and him being at a different point in his life. (Moran)

Together, they fly off on adventures, even as Rey protests that she must return home. "In the first stage of this kind of adventure, the hero leaves the realm of the familiar, over which he has some measure of control, and comes to a threshold" (Campbell and Moyers 146). Refusal of the call is a traditional step when faced with the unknown. Here, of course, her loyalty to her nebulous family contrasts with her duty to the galaxy – a common theme in *Star Wars*. When she flies for the first time "Rey felt Jakku trying to pull her back down," again, both literally and symbolically (Rucka, *Before the Awakening* 102).

> However, after she's proven she can outdo men in the arena of sports, warfare, or business, when she's gained external power and success, the Warrior Woman feels a spiritual lack. ... Deeper than she realizes is possible, a voice is calling her to find the Dark Goddess, the savage powerful icon of femininity, and absorb her wisdom. (Frankel, *Buffy* 8)

This is often less fairy godmother and more frightening death crone like Hecate, who helps Demeter on her own search. "This savage mentor offers the ultimate wisdom—the insight that darkness, mysticism, and even death are a woman's ultimate source of power, far different than a hero's outward force of arms" (Frankel, *Buffy* 8).

They fly to Takodana, where Rey is overwhelmed by the green of vibrant life. There, she meets the wise crone Maz Kanata. Her castle is a place of gathering and refuge, crowned by a statue of herself, welcoming all comers. Beside a lake, Maz's castle blends ancient stonework with modern sensor arrays and communication gear. "Maz enjoys this contrast. To her, it is yet another manifestation of a cosmic balance" (Hidalgo 73).

VALERIE ESTELLE FRANKEL

A mature woman, Maz calls Chewie her "boyfriend" and understands the world far better than innocent Rey. She's lived over a thousand years, becoming fully integrated with the natural world around her and boasting many feminine tools. She wears silver bracelets and belt buckle with a nature-link from her wooden beads. The keys at her belt are another feminine symbol, marking her as the lady and provider of the castle. She can feel the Force but only uses it subtly – she has no Jedi training and has never "walked that path herself, instead relying on her strong connection to the Force to keep her out of danger." (Hidalgo 72)

This perspective aids in her understanding, as she notes, "I have lived long enough to see the same eyes in different people." These eyes are how she understands the universe, while gigantic goggles emphasize her own seeing. In fact, glasses are a feminine tool of perception, emphasized by the magic spectacles and amber spyglass in *A Wrinkle in Time* and *The Amber Spyglass* respectively. Eyes, seeing, and being seen are a feminine power of cursing and perceiving throughout the world. "As an actor for films, your eyes are a lot of the way you communicate anyway," says her actor, Lupita Nyong'o. "So it was definitely a gift to have that be the means to her magic as a motion-capture character" (Breznican, *Star Wars*).

She tells Rey, "The Force, it's calling to you. Just let it in," as she guides her to a deeper understanding.

> Meeting Maz Kanata has a profound effect on Rey. She comes to understand that she is an essential part of a much larger galactic tapestry that is unfurling before her eyes and that the power of the Force is real. (Hidalgo 33)

Hearing the voice of her terrified younger self intruding on her consciousness, Rey heeds the call from her subconscious, with BB-8 beside her. As Campbell notes:

> The unconscious sends all sorts of vapors, odd beings, terrors and deluding images up into the mind—whether in

dream, broad daylight, or insanity; for the human kingdom, beneath the floor of the comparatively neat little dwelling that we call our consciousness, goes down into unexpected Aladdin caves. There not only jewels but also dangerous jinn abide: the inconvenient or resisted psychological powers that we have not thought or dared to integrate into our lives. (*Hero* 8)

She ventures into Maz's basement, where she finds Luke and Anakin's lightsaber. Taking it in this realm of buried and forgotten memories, Rey sees Cloud City and the rancor pit, as well as Luke's "No!" Luke lays his metal hand on R2-D2, while Yoda and Obi-Wan speak to Rey of her heritage. Ewan McGregor (Obi-Wan Kenobi in the prequel trilogy) tells her, "You've taken your first steps," while Alec Guiness (Obi-Wan Kenobi in the original trilogy) adds her name at the beginning. Abrams adds:

"I said, 'That's cool, is that the thing from Ewan McGregor?' He said 'No, we took a line from Alec Guinness saying 'Afraid.' They cut it, and you hear the performance – he's saying it the way I would have begged Alec Guinness to have said it. It is so crazy perfect. So when you hear Obi-Wan talk to Rey it is both Alec Guinness and Ewan McGregor doing the voice." (Anderton)

Thus all the mentors of the previous films, including now Luke, welcome her to her destiny. She also has a flashback to facing Kylo Ren as a child, after witnessing Luke put his hand on R2-D2 in the rain. Someone wearing a round helmet is about to strike her, then Kylo takes down this person with a lightsaber. Once Rey stands, she finds herself facing the Knights of Ren. Bodies of the young Jedi students Kylo and the Knights of Ren have killed surround them.

Maz comes to her in the basement, confronting her at the level below thought. With her deeper perception, not just of Rey but of the currents of the universe, she gives Rey a new mission:

Rey: I have to get back to Jakku.
Maz: Han told me. (takes her hands) Dear child, I see your eyes – you already know the truth. Whomever you are waiting for on Jakku, they're never coming back.
Rey cries.
Maz: But there's someone who still could.
Rey: Luke.
Maz: The belonging you seek is not behind you, it is ahead. I am no Jedi, but I know the force. It moves through and surrounds every living thing. Close your eyes, feel it. The light. It's always been there. It will guide you. The saber – take it.

The sword is a masculine tool, seen throughout the world's epics:

Most famous is Excalibur, though it has many companions: Lancelot's Arondight, Saint George's Ascalon, Roland's Durendal, Charlemagne's Flamberge, Paracelesus's Azoth, Siegfried's Gram, Muhammad's Zulfiqar, El Cid's Sword of Tizona, Beowulf 's Naegling, and Laevateinn—the sword Surtr will use to bring down the dome of heaven at Ragnarök. (Frankel, *From Girl to Goddess* 49)

Thus a sword is an unusual weapon for the heroine – a lightsaber that's a hybrid with Xena's chakram (a round distance weapon) or Buffy's scythe (the women's ancestral weapon of death) would be a more appropriate choice.

However, this gift links Rey with the legacy of Anakin and Luke and establishes that she's more suited for it than their heir, Kylo Ren. It carries with it Jedi status and tradition, the spirituality of blue, and the power of battle. Maz tells her, touching on the language from previous films, "That lightsaber was Luke's, and his father's before him and now it calls to you!"

Battling her legacy, Rey cries, "I'm never touching that thing again, I don't want any part of this." She runs away into "a primordial forest seemingly never touched by technology" (Hidalgo 73) in a second refusal of the call. The forest represents the deep mystical, the feminine power the heroine from the desert has never absorbed. It shelters and protects her. BB-8 comes after her and whimpers at her to rejoin the quest, but she refuses. At this point, Rey hesitates on her spiritual journey, and it takes the shocking murders of the entire Hosnian system to galvanize her into action.

Worse yet, Ren invades her forest sanctuary, following her into a narrow cleft. With the music and angle, it's reminiscent of Luke facing Vader in the cave on Dagobah. In the "innermost cave" as Campbell put it, the chosen one is tested, tempted with power. Only the strongest can reject the easy solution. Like Luke, Rey is suppressing the truth of her origin and destiny. When she refuses to face it, it intrudes on her in the wilderness of the unconscious world. Ren demands BB-8. Rey refuses and he carries her off. Only her innocence (BB-8) remains.

The enemy too may progress through Animus stages – Rey easily defeats the brutal scavengers and thugs on Jakku, where she's trained all her life to battle such adversaries. But the New Order, itself a force of order and law (obviously), defeats her, Finn, and Han on Jakku. Her friends' impulsive lack of planning is no match for the Order's long-arranged scheme, and General Hux uses Starkiller Base to destroy the New Republic. As he dictates to rows and rows of disciplined troops:

> Today is the end of the Republic. The end of a regime that acquiesces to disorder. At this very moment in a system far from here, the New Republic lies to the galaxy while secretly supporting the treachery of the rogues of the Resistance. This fierce machine which you have built, upon which we stand will bring an end to the Senate, to their cherished fleet. All remaining systems will bow to the First Order and will remember this as the last day of the Republic!

Snoke and the New Order are the destroyers, savagery incarnate and killers of innocent life that the heroine is sworn to protect. Most male villains in the classic heroine's story take this role. In fact the novelization further emphasizes their savagery as Snoke and General Hux plot to kill millions to forward their schemes:

> The redheaded officer spoke up immediately. "I do have a proposition. The weapon. We have it. It is ready. I believe the time has come to use it."
> "Against?"
> "The Republic. Or what its fractious proponents choose to call the Republic. Their center of government, its entire system. In the chaos that will follow, the Resistance will have no choice but to investigate an attack of such devastating scale. They will throw all their resources into trying to discover its source. So they have no choice but to investigate fully, and in so doing..."
> "Reveal themselves."
> Snoke was clearly pleased.
> "And if they don't... we've destroyed them."
> "Yes," Snoke said in satisfaction. "Extreme. Audacious. I agree that the time for such measures has come. Go. Oversee the necessary preparations."

In this type of story pattern, the entire universe reflects Rey, and her friends are sides of her personality. Thus she takes a painful blow with the capital's destruction.

Phasma works with the New Order, but as she has given her personality, identity, and will over to the patriarchy, she is the "evil matriarch" and brainwasher of young children. Often the heroine studies with such a mentor: Katniss and President Coin, Buffy and Professor Walsh, Lyra and her mother in *The Golden Compass,* fairytales' evil stepmothers. All these allow the heroine to understand powerful women in the male hierarchy. The heroines, however, reject such a role, absorbing the lessons from this kind of power, but choosing instead to work in the service of life and comradeship. While this is a traditional step, in this adventure Phasma and Rey do not interact. Rey's adversary is Kylo Ren, emphasizing once more her path on a more masculine adventure.

A higher level of Animus arrives with the entire Resistance fleet, the last remaining orderly structure of good. With them is General Leia Organa, replacing the male hierarchy with a strong female and giving Rey a new kind of role model who can teach her the next stage of growth. Rey is not present in the scene, but the audience functions as her stand in, as the next stage of power on Rey's quest appears.

Leia is the ruling queen of the Rebellion (symbolically and basically literally), but also a mother – in fact, a bereft one. She has the next level of wisdom to offer Rey – how to bear suffering and loss while fighting for the greater cause of the universe. She makes the tough choices, including sending in Han to save Ben.

Campbell explains that in classic tales, "the hero is swallowed and taken into the abyss to be later resurrected – a variant of the death-and-resurrection theme" (Campbell and Moyers 146). The hero descends into the underworld or the darkest place of all, like Frodo into Mordor or Harry Potter into the mirror chamber where he faces Voldemort. In the Innermost Cave, the hero often dies only to return more powerful. This is a metaphor for undergoing a crisis and emerging stronger, armed with the wisdom of adulthood.

The heroine sometimes follows this pattern, but she has her own variants. At the climax of the Innermost Cave, the questing heroine often falls into a magic sleep, like Snow White or Sleeping Beauty. This allows her a cocoon-like transformation between one stage of being and another – usually childhood and adulthood.

> Snow White lies unconscious, perfectly preserved in glass, but at the same time, the coffin is like a crucible, transforming her from frightened child into powerful queen. This sleep, of course, symbolizes the heroine's descent into death, where she must confront her mortality and gain wisdom from the experience. When she wakes, she has become stronger. (Frankel, *From Girl to Goddess* 30).

Katniss falls into madness and drug-induced hospitalization at the end of each book, emphasizing her working through her trauma and absorbing its new lessons. In Rey's case, her flight into the forest shows her panic at an entire past life of family and Jedi skills, as well as its menacing enemy, Kylo Ren. When she encounters him in the forest, he knocks her unconscious, symbolically allowing her to progress to her next level of maturity, after absorbing the horrors of her past.

Kylo Ren then carries off Rey and imprisons her in a torture chamber. This place is far outside of Rey's comfort zone, symbolized especially by the ice world surrounding the desert girl.

> Journeying here represents the heroine leaving the place of her feminine power to ascend to the prince's tower or mountain, where she faces her greatest trial far from her unconscious realm of magic. The Little Mermaid leaves the ocean and Demeter leaves her fields as both journey into the man's world—human civilization. If Buffy's school library or home is invaded, that suggests an assault on Buffy's self. But when she journeys into the enemy's sphere, she's alone and vulnerable, cut off from her strongest supports. (Frankel, *Buffy* 60)

Despite her isolation, the heroine battles with inner strength. Back on the Starkiller Base, Rey faces Kylo Ren, now tougher with the power of order. "You know I can do whatever I want," he taunts her and reads her mind, invading her private thoughts. The ocean and island in her mind are her destiny – Luke Skywalker, but also an image of feminine fertility and natural power, now brutalized by the patriarchy.

She fights back, reading his mind in turn and using his training and discipline against him. "You're afraid. That you will never be as strong as Darth Vader," she sees, understanding the patriarchy's inherent weakness, that it's a hierarchy with the most powerful on top and thus always a constant struggle. Though the Destroyer seems all-powerful, there's insecurity beneath. Like Kylo Ren, Snoke's megalomania conceals deep-held dread. The novelization reveals that Snoke fears Luke Skywalker and plans to destroy an entire system so no one finds where Luke is, himself included.

In fact, when the heroine confronts the tyrant and refuses

to give in, he crumbles.

> On the heroine's journey, the young questor comes to realize that she is mightier than the tyrant: Dorothy cowers before the "Great and Powerful Oz" when she reaches his Emerald City. But after facing the far more terrifying Wicked Witch of the West, she grows into someone strong enough to kick over the Wizard's pasteboard head and confront the fraud cowering behind it. Katniss too realizes that the Capitol's *threat* far outweighs the Capitol itself. As she declares on one of her broadcasts: "The Capitol's fragile because it depends on the districts for everything. Food, energy, even the Peacekeepers that police us. If we declare our freedom, the Capitol collapses. President Snow, thanks to you, I'm officially declaring mine today" (*Mockingjay* 169). Like their broken electric fences, the Capitol has only the illusion of authority, until Katniss can shatter it. At series end, she meets Snow heavily shackled and helpless in his rose garden and knows she can kill him. (Frankel, *Many Faces of Katniss* 117)

Her encounters with Ren give her the necessary knowledge. After this, she masters the "Force trick" and controls the orderly yet obedient Stormtroopers. The "First Order" are no match for her will:

> Rey: You will remove these restraints and leave this cell with the door open.
> Stormtrooper: What did you say?
> Rey: You will remove these restraints and leave this cell with the door open.
> Stormtrooper: I will tighten these restraints, scavenger scum!
> Rey: (more pacifically) You will remove these restraints and leave this cell with the door open.
> Stormtrooper: I will remove these restraints and leave this cell with the door open.
> [he does so]
> Rey: And you will drop your weapon.
> Stormtrooper: And I'll drop my weapon.

Finn comes to save her on the ship, though she's already saved herself. There's a romantic moment as they embrace, one that's been building through the show as he tries to take her with him far from the war and tells her pleadingly, "You looked at me like no one ever had." This romance is a vital step on the journey, though each time it usually takes the same form.

> Shapeshifting lovers are common figures in myth, from swan maidens to frog princes. "We have all experienced relationships in which our partner is fickle, two-faced, bewilderingly changeable," Vogler explains (65). The hero's or heroine's lover is incomprehensible, shifting moods and desires faster than the protagonist can comprehend. The task is to penetrate these shapes and barriers, to find the true self within. Only then can a pair fully commit. (Frankel, *Buffy* 26)

Finn introduces himself to Rey as a fighter for the Resistance. Only in Maz's castle does he reveal all this has been a lie: "I'm not Resistance. I'm a Stormtrooper," he admits. She accepts this and allows him to transform into another person, one more determined to flee the First Order than fight for freedom. They have opposing missions now, which are certain to part them:

> Finn: Come with me.
> Rey: Don't go.

When Finn invades the heart of the First Order to save her, he has transformed again, this time into a true hero, worthy of her love.

The heroine then faces death – the ultimate test. Rey's isn't her own but Han's by Kylo Ren's evil hand. Like Lucy and Susan of Narnia, who witness Aslan shaved, mocked, and murdered, humbled before them, Rey thus discovers her father-figure's helplessness to protect her – she must rely on herself.

> The classic heroine learns independence, not protection from her father-figure. Lyra of *The Golden Compass* discovers that her father is a murderer when he

> kills her helpless friend Roger. Meg Murray crosses time and space to rescue her blinded and confused father, and they tesseract to a friendly planet. When Meg demands that he return to rescue her brother Charles Wallace, Meg's three witch mentors appear and tell Meg her father is not powerful enough. Meg gazes sadly at him. "I wanted you to do it all for me...I was scared, and I didn't want to have to do anything myself" (L'Engle 187). With this, she acknowledges she is the only one who can rescue Charles Wallace, so she returns to confront the monstrous IT.
>
> Cinna, Boggs, Finnick, and Katniss's father die, Gale is whipped in the square, and then he and Beetee are revealed as accidental masterminds behind Prim's death. Peeta is hijacked. In the course of the series, all the powerful males in Katniss's life, from mentors to friends, lose their power. (Frankel, *Many Faces of Katniss* 118)

At Han's tragic murder, the entire universe seems to pause. Then while Chewie, representing her inner primitive violence, erupts with anger, she and Finn flee into the snow, now surrounded by darkness and explosions.

The hero flees into the mysterious forest to connect with his lost feminine side – spirituality and wisdom. The heroine goes there to find her true place and her power. This time the forest is dark and filled with explosions from Ren's base. Once again, Ren invades her sanctuary in pursuit of her. After he knocks her unconscious once more and savages Finn, she takes up Luke's lightsaber at last. As it flies to her hand, it confirms her destiny. Luke's beloved theme music plays. Like Luke and many warrior women, she is on the hero's journey at this moment, seeking to topple the Dark Lord and save the galaxy.

Rey's battle with Kylo Ren in their lightsaber duel is empowering. The same audio as the beginning of the battle between Luke and Vader in *Jedi* emphasizes her similar mission – to rid the galaxy of a tyrant, however she must. "You need a teacher. I can show you the ways of the Force," he offers. However, she rejects this condescending invitation to submit. She breathes, commanding calm, and then turns on him, wounding him repeatedly then beating him.

> It's Kylo Ren who discovers how powerful she is, that she is his superior both mentally and physically, and it scares him. (She's also much less prone to fits of rage, which has its benefits.) In Ren's last-ditch effort to lure her over to the dark side we feel his desperation at being outmatched. Their final battle, in the snow, is all about good and evil. It's never about physical strength, and it's never about gender. (Sperling)

However, as Luke finds on facing Vader, there's also a spiritual challenge. The novelization portrays it thus: "*Kill him*, a voice inside her head said. It was amorphous, unidentifiable, raw. Pure vengeful emotion. So *easy*, she told herself. So *quick*." Instead of killing him, Rey "recoil[s]" from the feeling, rejecting the pull of the dark side.

She lets his chaotic world crumble away, as a ravine splits and fire begins to consume the land. Instead, she saves Finn and returns to the Resistance with Chewie. There, Leia greets and embraces her without a word. Rey has chosen the side of goodness and spiritual growth and thus is accepted by the good mother, the matriarch who nonetheless knows that sacrifices are necessary. In the novelization, she has a longer goodbye with Rey:

> "I'm proud of what you're about to do," she told the girl.
> Rey replied in all seriousness. "But you're also afraid. In sending me away, you're—reminded."
> Leia straightened. "You won't share the fate of our son."
> "I know what we're doing is right. This is how it has to be. This is how it should be."
> Leia smiled gently, reassuringly. "I know it, too. May the Force be with you."

With the gift of R2-D2's map, Rey sets out on the final stage of her quest. Save for Chewie, still a guide to the primitive natural world, she goes alone, back to her basic wooden staff. Leia's "May the Force be with you," is her final send off, the mother's blessing to the young heroine's setting out. At the mysterious world of water and ocean, another place of fertile green and lifesaving water, she climbs the hill, finds Luke Skywalker, and gives him the lightsaber.

The Animus in its highest stage "gives the woman spiritual firmness, an invisible inner support that compensates for her outer softness" (Von Franz, "The Process of Individuation" 194). This is Luke, presumably destined to become her mentor in true wisdom. Having conquered the journey's many stages, she's finally ready to undergo her own training.

While some of the points are feminine, she has predominantly mastered the *hero's* journey, defeating the Dark Lord with (possibly) her father's sword, and gathering a band of friends who can teach her masculine skills. Now, with female mentors and more training in perception, she must grow along the steps of the heroine's in order to find wholeness.

FINN'S HERO'S JOURNEY

While Rey's journey has more than a trace of hero in it, Finn's has something of the heroine's: More problematically, all his acts, from trying to rescue his ladylove to confronting his evil parent, have more than a trace of farce. He's a hero, but more subverted than mythic.

His call to adventure comes when turning away from war – his friend is injured, he and his team are ordered to shoot civilians, and he's disgusted. "On my first battle, I made a choice: I wasn't going to kill for them. So I ran," he insists in the film. *The Visual Dictionary* comments that FN-2187 "lacks the combat zeal or submission to authority evident in his squadmates" but "keeps his misgivings well hidden" (Hidalgo 20). On his first mission, tested at last, he chooses.

A female drill sergeant and mentor is certainly unusual for the soldier story as well as for the hero's journey. Captain Phasma suggests a mother figure rather than a father one, but is distant and cruel in an inversion of the trope. In Finn's prequel book, Captain Phasma scolds him for compassion as he aids fellow teammates like the clumsy Slip. She tells him:

> You have great potential, 2187. You are officer corps material. Your duty is to the First Order above everything. Nothing else comes before that. FN-2003 must stand or fall on his own. If he stands, the Order is strengthened. If he falls, the Order is spared his weakness. Am I understood? (Rucka, *Before the Awakening* 55)

When he goes easy on Slip in the combat ring, Phasma sends him on the village raid for a final chance to prove himself

On returning onscreen to the ship, she never unmasks, emphasizing her role as the faceless authority. In fact, she demands he replace his own mask, symbolically abandoning his traces of individual personality. Building on this, she threatens to recondition him and he flees. With the help of a new friend, he chooses a new life for himself, leaving his familiar world behind.

In the process, he saves a person in trouble, much as Rey saves BB-8. He whisks a handcuffed Poe Dameron into an alcove and offers to rescue him as they escape together in a TIE fighter. This act of aid is not altruistic, however, but expedient, in another subversion of the great ideals someone like Luke Skywalker has:

> Poe Dameron: Why are you helping me?
> Finn: Because it's the right thing to do.
> Poe Dameron: ...you need a pilot.
> Finn: I need a pilot.

Despite this start, Poe offers Finn a true friendship, independent of the Stormtrooper lifestyle. He is a companion reflecting part of Finn he's never explored – the smart-talking comedian or trickster. The Trickster's main function is to "bring about healthy change and transformation, often by drawing attention to the imbalance or absurdity of a stagnant psychological situation" as the natural enemy of the status quo, Vogler explains (77). As a Rebel pilot, his life is devoted to freedom and choice. His presence awakens Finn to a world outside the Stormtrooper agenda, one of defending innocents rather than destroying them.

He also gives Finn the gift of a name, indicator of individual personality. As they fly off together, Finn leaves his past behind forever.

> In contrast with Finn and Rey's youthful kindred-spirit bond, Finn and Poe share a kind of fierce joy as they escape the Star Destroyer, later reuniting at the Resistance base on D'Qar. (Baker-Whitelaw)

They crash onto Jakku and Poe vanishes, leaving Finn with nothing. On Jakku, Poe's first talisman is Poe's jacket – a masculine tool, indeed. Nonetheless, clothing is most often a gift for the heroine, from magic cloaks to slippers to gowns. When the male hero gets such an item, he's a gentle hero, meant to use the gifts in pacifism and cleverness – turning invisible rather than fighting.

> Clothes-sharing has long been a symbol of intimacy, and here it's plot-relevant as well. Poe's jacket is what draws BB-8 to Finn on Jakku and sets in motion their intergalactic adventure. It may also be Finn's first true possession, a gift that feels all the more meaningful when he later lends it to Rey. (Baker-Whitelaw)

BB-8 is another talisman, complete with feminine roundness. Adventuring with BB-8 and Chewie, Finn learns to accept those different from himself, even those who speak a language he can't understand. Finn builds on the new name Poe gave him to forge a completely new identity: Resistance "Big Deal" Finn on a mission to deliver the droid and save Luke Skywalker. In fact, he and Rey protect BB-8 like two parents with a child, showing him a new possible role for his future.

Rey is his link to the feminine, though as an independent fighter, mechanic, and pilot, she seems more of a gateway to masculine skills. He clutches her hand, she orders him to stop. As she calls for tools on the Falcon and he fumbles to choose the right ones, his own lack of traditional male talents comes to the forefront. Being around her awakens feelings of love, but as with Katniss and Peeta, he is the more sensitive one and more eager in the relationship, while she's spent a lifetime building toughness and reserve. Thus the classic roles are flipped once more.

On Maz Kanata's planet, Finn finally tells her the truth of himself: "I'm not Resistance. I'm a Stormtrooper." Rey unconditionally accepts this, and he's emboldened to proclaim his love, at least subtly, telling her, "You looked at me like no one ever had." He wants Rey, but even more, he wants to escape. "I'm done with the First Order. I'm never going back," he vows. Now they're advancing on the planet.

He nearly leaves Takodana in a life-changing refusal of the call, but relents when Rey is in danger. His heart in his eyes, he asks, "Where's Rey?" then screams with despair when Kylo Ren takes her onto his ship and flies away. At last he chooses a side, even if it's for love, not duty. Maz gives him the lightsaber, but her line, "Take it – find your friend" emphasizes that the sword of Jedi heritage is meant for Rey, not Finn.

At the Resistance Base, Finn is celebrated for his knowledge and training. For the first time, he's completely himself, not pretending to be a killer Stormtrooper or a brave Resistance leader. In fact, his working in sanitation can save the day. However, he goes along on the mission to save his girl, and in a subversive twist, she rescues herself without him. Worse yet, he's not the hero who can dismantle Starkiller Base, only a young man looking for his love. Han is horrified that Finn lied about his abilities:

> Han: The galaxy is counting on us!
> Finn: So? We'll figure it out.

To Finn, love ranks above the mission, the Resistance, or the galaxy itself, though he does muddle through after all.

As it turns out, his further plan involves revenge on his hated Captain Phasma, though this takes a comical turn:

> Finn: My name's Finn. I'm in charge! I'm in charge now, Phasma! I'm in charge!
> Han: Bring it down…bring it down…

In her day-to-day life, Phasma has decided to gain power in the world of men by learning to dominate them. All the Stormtroopers must follow her commands as she trains and even reconditions them in the ultimate display of control. Her Animus rules her personality. "A woman with a highly developed animus becomes overly aggressive, intellectual, and power-hungry" (Zweig 188). Nonetheless, she is an unusual adversary for the hero, whose mother figure is usually closer to kindly Aunt Beru. She is a more common mentor and adversary for the heroine. Nonetheless, this time the hero confronts her. Finn, the Stormtrooper with the heart of a pacifist, wants to beat Phasma but also reject every part of her and cast her from himself. While she surrenders quite quickly onscreen, in the book, Chewbacca and Han get rougher:

> She managed a slight shake of her head. "Even a Wookiee can't crush First Order armor." In response, Chewbacca tightened his grip further. Her mask emitted a slight but perceptible wheeze.
> "Well," Han said nonchalantly, "there's one way to find out."

Either way, he takes his revenge at last: his nemesis has been banished from his consciousness as she vanishes from sight in *Star Wars* tradition:

> Finn: [asking about Phasma] What should we do with her?
> Han Solo: Is there a garage chute... or trash compactor?

This is far from the Darth-Vader-Luke-Skywalker duel that emphasizes their rage and power alongside the complex nuances of love, hate, and admiration. As he gloats, Finn sounds like a triumphant child with leverage. Thus his moment of glory as he takes the power back from his longtime nemesis is more goofy than profound. He's rewarded with a hug from his rescued love, though Han breaks this up with "Escape now, hug later."

> *The Force Awakens* wisely steered clear of any overt romance between the new characters, although there are some hints of it in earlier scenes between Finn and Rey, like Finn grabbing Rey's hand and later asking if Rey has a boyfriend. But this could just as easily be a case of Finn reaching out for human contact after a lifetime encased in the chilly confines of a stormtrooper uniform. Honestly,

there's already a similar capacity for romance between Finn and Poe, although it's illustrated in a more symbolic fashion. (Baker-Whitelaw)

The kisses Leia gave Luke in the first two films were more overt, though given how the pair turned out, it's not surprising *Star Wars* is holding back a little this time. Rey and Finn may be related too in the end. In Campbell's hero's journey, the heroine is the hero's prize and also a guide to the softer side of the self – spirituality, understanding, and emotion. Through his love for Rey, Finn finds all these but also a much larger connection to the more classically masculine element of duty as he becomes a Resistance fighter at last.

Joseph Campbell notes that this descent is common to all cultures, and to all genders: There's the inner quest and the outer:

> In the first stage of this kind of adventure, the hero leaves the realm of the familiar, over which he has some measure of control, and comes to a threshold, let us say, the edge of a lake or sea, where a monster of the abyss comes to meet him.
> There are then two possibilities. In a story of the Jonah type, the hero is swallowed and taken into the abyss to be later resurrected—a variant of the death-and-resurrection theme. The conscious personality here has come in touch with a charge of unconscious energy which it is unable to handle and must now suffer all the trials and revelations of a terrifying night-sea journey, while learning how to come to terms with this power of the dark and emerge, at last, to a new way of life.
> The other possibility is that the hero, on encountering the power of the dark, may overcome and kill it, as did Siegfried and St. George when they killed the dragon. But as Siegfried learned, he must then taste the dragon blood, in order to take to himself some of that dragon power. When Siegfried has killed the dragon and tasted the blood, he hears the song of nature. He has transcended his humanity and reassociated himself with the powers of nature, which are the powers of our life, and from which our minds remove us. (Campbell and Moyers 146)

Rey is shown undergoing both journeys, first in the basement, then battling Kylo Ren in the forest. But Finn does not confront his missing self in the darkness, and his battles with Captain Phasma and Kylo Ren are short and superficial – he isn't shown being temped, mentally tested, or otherwise "tasting the dragon power" – he simply threatens Phasma and loses to Ren.

In the forest, Finn battles Kylo Ren with a lightsaber to save his unconscious friend. However, the film soon reveals that he was really Rey's temporary stand-in. The lightsaber flies to her hand and she trounces the supervillain. After his clumsy battle and her more epic one, Rey and Chewie must pick up his unconscious body and carry him off. After all his attempts to rescue Rey, he's become the damsel.

Finn ends the film still unconscious, with Rey bidding him a touching farewell. She kisses him and says, "We will meet again soon, my friend. Thank you, my friend." This is a descent into death (or near death) for the hero. Presumably he'll return next film, wiser from his adventure. Nonetheless, he's robbed of a great deal of agency as he misses the film's ending.

Through it all, he's been the accidental hero, the one who runs away instead of fighting, and when he does fight, the one who misses the mark. He's like a more earnest version of Han Solo, not a Luke Skywalker. Nonetheless, he follows many of the classic steps in his own way, however subverted.

DIVERSITY ARRIVES IN THE COUNTDOWN TO THE FORCE AWAKENS BOOKS

Claudia Gray's YA novel *Lost Stars* follows two children, Thane Kyrell and Ciena Ree, as they attend the Imperial Academy on Coruscant together. She becomes a pilot, while he grows disillusioned and finally joins the Rebellion, leaving the pair as star-crossed lovers observing the events of the first trilogy. Nonetheless, there are more roles for women in the new lineup than young lovers. The Countdown to *The Force Awakens* lineup includes bounty hunters, assassins, and scavengers.

There are even space-moms. Rebel pilot Norra Wexley and her tech-wiz son Temmin star in *Aftermath*, while Poe's parents both fight for the Empire – his father on the ground, his mother in the sky. In the comic *Shattered Empire*, his mother Shara Bey flies Leia off to liberate Naboo, then aids Luke on his own quest. He finally gives her the Force-sensitive tree that grows at the center of the Jedi Temple on Coruscant. She takes it and settles down on Yavin 4 with her family. Poe grows up riding in her ship at the start of his own prequel story, dreaming of being like her someday.

Maz herself seems a grandmotherly figure, already a thousand years old, but she only acts as hostess for other characters, rather than starring in her own tale. It seems she's keeping her secrets.

AHSOKA

Ahsoka Tano, a Togruta female, is the Padawan learner to Anakin Skywalker and a fighter in the movie and television show *The Clone Wars*. While she begins as Anakin's sidekick, she gains a great deal of agency. She becomes a true warrior, aiding in key Republic victories like the Second Battle of Geonosis and the Battle of Mon Cala. In season three she undergoes the heroine's journey arc, dying and returning in the mystical Jedi realm of Mortis. She's a mentor to the next generation, helping Jedi children and freeing slaves.

In the fifth season, Tano is framed for the bombing of the Jedi Temple hangar and she loses faith in the system. Instead of seeking traditional justice, she flees into the Coruscant underworld to clear her name. There, she finds herself working with Asajj Ventress. This alien woman is a Force-sensitive Nightsister, powerful and loyal in her own way. Ultimately, Anakin bursts into her trial and clears Tano. However, the Jedi Order's lack of faith in her has traumatized her, and, devastated, she leaves them forever.

In *Star Wars: Rebels,* she finally reveals herself as Rebel intelligence officer Fulcrum, who connects all the cells. She has additional growth as she discovers to her horror that her old friend and master has become Darth Vader. Through both series she's an iconic character, the cool alien and Jedi who's also female.

HERA

Hera Syndulla is a Twi'lek female rebel and an amazing pilot in the sequel series, *Star Wars: Rebels*. While she's not the teen hero of the story, she does get to act like the bossy older sister, ordering young Ezra off her ship to run errands. Though she doesn't have major story arcs, she's well-schooled in the ways of the Rebel Alliance and provides the intelligence for her team.

SABINE

The human Sabine, also on *Star Wars: Rebels,* has the gender-bending role of weapons expert. Even more unusually for action shows, she's an artist. Her great joy is spraying Imperial propaganda with graffiti – generally of her chosen symbol, a starbird – her personal sigil eventually becomes the symbol of the Rebellion. She cheerily mocks the white clad Stormtroopers in their white TIE fighters, giving it all a dash of dazzling rainbow with paint bombs. With sarcastic quipping and a feature-concealing suit of Mandalorian armor that she's heavily customized, she's anything but dull.

FARNAY

Luke's prequel book *The Weapon of a Jedi* has a large female presence. In fact, C3PO tells Luke's story to fighter pilot Jess Testor. In it there's another interesting heroine.

On the planet Devaron, Luke meets Farnay, a mechanic's daughter. A brave young adolescent, she's a typical Devaron inhabitant – as they lose their agrarian lifestyle for the modern age, thanks to Imperial bullying. She's a "scavenger," significantly.

She saves his life, defending him with a pistol and helping after he's knocked out. After, he promises to come back and restore the Jedi order and the temple they found together. When he returns she's "grown into quite a capable young woman" according to Threepio, who adds that the story will have to wait (Fry, *Weapon of a Jedi* 184). Is this Rey's mother?

SANA

Sana appears in the new comic book series (which takes place between *A New Hope* and *Empire Strikes Back*). Uncompromisingly nasty in a face-concealing mask, she shoots the denizens of Tatooine until they give her information. After tracking Han Solo across the galaxy for undisclosed reasons, she finally finds him hiding in the Monsua Nebula with Leia, on a planet surrounded by fierce electrical storms.

Sana dramatically interrupts them both during a quiet moment and announces herself saying, "He'd just lie. It's the only thing he's ever been good at. I should know. The name is Sana Solo. I'm his wife" (#6).

Though Han denies it, Sana insists she has paperwork.

One reviewer notes, "Since Marvel's *Star Wars* comics – which are considered canon – recently revealed Han Solo had a secret wife, the beautiful dark-skinned Sana, maybe Finn is really Han's (imagine how annoyed the smuggler would be to have a son as a Stormtrooper)" ("In the Shadow" 92).

While Leia announces the situation is none of her business, Sana realizes there's a bounty on Leia and has her associate destroy their shuttle. Now she can turn Leia over to the Imperials and bring Solo back with her.

Though Leia turns a weapon on her, Han is still in trouble. He insists to Leia that their marriage was just part of a con – they needed to throw a big ceremony as part of it and a wedding fit the bill. "It had to look real…it had to pretty much be…" he adds sheepishly. "But it wasn't…I mean, I never actually…" (#11).

Issue twelve finally concludes matters: Rescuing Luke on Tatooine, Leia and Sana are separated from the others, and Sana is trapped under rocks. Leia, wielding her saber, cuts through them to rescue the other woman. Sana, surprised that Leia had come back from her, finally tells her the truth – that marrying Han had been part of a scam and she's only seeking her cut. This is a rather light story to be drawn out for six issues – one wonders whether there really is more to come. Either way, a butt-kicking female bounty hunter has entered the mythos, adding to the number of Black people in the galaxy.

BAZINE

In Maz's cantina, there's a corpulent alien cuddled up with a thin woman. In an inversion of the Jabba-Princess Leia dynamic, however, she's a spy for the Empire exploiting him rather than being exploited. Grummgar is the stooge to pirate Bazine Netal, who wears a complex pattern of black and white striped diamonds made of "sensor jamming baffleweave" (Hidalgo 74). Her dagger is angled and bent as herself…and poisoned.

The Countdown short story "The Perfect Weapon" gives

her a unique tale. It begins:

> The night was young, and Bazine Netal was hunting. Curled up on a stool in formfitting black that matched her eyes, lips, and hair, she scanned the room for her contact and found only fools.

She is always on her guard, always contemptuous of those around her, especially the men. While she casually puts down all those who make advances, she often follows up her words with "one simple but elegant kick" that strikes nerve clusters and puts the men down longer. Other tools include a gallery of disguises.

In the story she's hired to retrieve a steel case from a Clone trooper. However, she runs afoul of her own trainer and father figure Kloda who proves he's one more man not to be trusted. Despite her coldness, the story finds a way to show the vulnerable woman within and offer some empathy.

KOR SELLA

Korr Sella (played by Maisie Richardson-Sellers) was meant to have an arc in the film as Leia's emissary. Sadly, this had to be cut, presumably for time, and now she only appears as the lovely Black woman seen standing on a balcony, gazing up in horror as the First Order wipes out the Hosnian solar system. The novelization keeps her scene:

> As usual, Leia did not waste time on small talk: "You need to go to the Senate right away. Tell them I insist that they take action against the First Order. The longer they bicker and delay, the stronger the Order becomes." She leaned toward the other woman. "If they fail to take action soon, the Order will have grown so strong the Senate will be unable to do anything. It won't matter what they think."
> Sella indicated her understanding. "With all respect: Do you think the senators will listen?"
> "I don't know." Leia bit down on her lower lip. "So much time has passed. There was a time when they were at least willing to listen. And of course, the Senate's makeup has changed. Some of those who were always willing to pay

attention to me have retired. Some of those who have replaced them have their own agendas." She smiled ruefully. "Not all senators think I'm crazy. Or maybe they do. I don't care what they think about me as long as they take action."

The emissary nodded. "I'll do all I can to ensure the Resistance gets the hearing we deserve. But why don't you go yourself, General? An appeal of this nature is always more effective when delivered firsthand."

Leia's smile thinned. "I might make it to the Senate, yes. I might even be able to deliver my speech. But I would never, never get out of the Hosnian system alive. I would have a terrible 'accident,' or become the victim of some 'deranged' radical. Or I would eat something that didn't agree with me. Or encounter someone who didn't agree with me." She composed herself. "I have total confidence in you, Sella. I know you will deliver our message to the full extent of your considerable abilities." The emissary smiled back, grateful for the confidence the general was expressing."

Tragically, she dies before she can make the Senate see sense.

SINJIR

Building on all this diversity, the universe now has same-sex romance. In *Star Wars: Aftermath,* two gay couples are casually mentioned, as "the Rebel fighter Norra Wexley, one of the main characters in *Aftermath,* has an older sister named Esmelle, who agrees that she and her wife, Shirene, will watch over Norra's son while she is off fighting" (Cox). Further, hero Sinjir Rath politely declines the character Jas's advances because he is "not into" women. Chuck Wendig, the author, said of LucasFilm:

> They have been very gracious and accommodating for that sort of thing, as they should be. The only question in terms of story stuff was, some of the earlier readers of the book were like, well, it's kind of a shame, because he and that other character actually have some good chemistry. So in some ways it's like, well, it's a shame that they're not getting together

[...] I don't think that his sexuality needs to be this giant plot point, but at the same time, it's part of who he is as a character, and I thought it was an interesting moment. Especially since you don't necessarily see it as much – not just in *Star Wars* but just in science-fiction. (Cox)

He adds that there's been a little backlash, which in his opinion completely misses the point: "If you can imagine a world where Luke Skywalker would be irritated that there were gay people around him, you completely missed the point of *Star Wars*" (Cox).

A REY OF HOPE

FEMINIST SUBVERSIONS

LUKE SKYWALKER HAS VANISHED. IN HIS ABSENCE, THE SINISTER FIRST ORDER HAS RISEN FROM THE ASHES OF THE EMPIRE AND WILL NOT REST UNTIL SKYWALKER, THE LAST JEDI, HAS BEEN DESTROYED.

WITH THE SUPPORT OF THE REPUBLIC, GENERAL LEIA ORGANA LEADS A BRAVE RESISTANCE. SHE IS DESPERATE TO FIND HER BROTHER LUKE AND GAIN HIS HELP IN RESTORING PEACE AND JUSTICE TO THE GALAXY.

LEIA HAS SENT HER MOST DARING PILOT ON A SECRET MISSION TO JAKKU, WHERE AN OLD ALLY HAS DISCOVERED A CLUE TO LUKE'S WHEREABOUTS . . .

In itself this title sequence more than provides the exposition. It sets up a new kind of story with a shift in who gets to be front and center.

Luke is gone. In fact, he won't be the hero-leader of the story at all. All of the other characters will make a new narrative and show what they have to contribute, front and center. The second paragraph introduces "General Leia

Organa" – no longer Princess Leia and not Mrs. Leia Solo either. She is the active one as she organizes the search, while Luke remains passive, waiting to be found. In fact, Luke doesn't have a single line in the film, only waiting as active Rey sets out to find him, much as Princess Leia waited the first time around. "Leia is in need of finding in *A New Hope*, so Luke is in need of finding in *The Force Awakens*" (VanDerWerff). In the book, Rey's thoughts provide a fun callback to this switchover:

> His hair and beard were white, and his countenance was haunted. He did not speak, nor did she.
> Remembering, Rey reached into her pack and removed his Lightsaber. Taking several steps forward, she held it out to him. An offer. A plea. The galaxy's only hope.

All this sets the scene for a far different *Star Wars* universe, one that's been changing for a while:

> There has been a noticeable increase of prominent women in *Star Wars*; most notably with Ahsoka and Ventress in *Star Wars: The Clone Wars*, and Hera and Sabine in *Star Wars Rebels*. But in these cartoons they are still supporting players in Anakin and Ezra's stories. They are most certainly included, even at times emphasized, and in the case of Ahsoka receive a great amount of development, but they are never the character who's central to the story. (Moran)

Certainly, there have been strong women in *Star Wars* (well, two of them) with more in the less-popular television shows and novelizations. However, women's roles in the franchise have always been sidelined. Certainly, Leia was bold and powerful in her time: When attacked by Stormtroopers in her first scene, the senator in modest white with giant hair buns snatches a blaster. She even shoots first. Unleashing her powerful tongue while imprisoned by the Empire, she mocks them all with "Darth Vader, only you could be so bold," "Governor Tarkin, I should have expected to find you holding Vader's leash. I recognized your foul stench when I was brought on board," and the memorable, "Aren't you a little short for a Stormtrooper?"

Billie Lourd says, "When I noticed the movie for the first time, I noticed my mom was not only as confident and strong as the men, she was one of the most confident characters in the entire film. It made me realize women are just as powerful as men and that we can truly do anything they can (if not more)" ("Billie Lourd," 52).

> While Han Solo shirks responsibility and Luke Skywalker fumbles around with his evolving, boyish perception of the hero, Leia gets things done. When her own rescue goes awry, she grabs the blaster herself and finds a way out. She's not just a princess but a radical fighting for freedom under a tyrannical empire.
>
> "She had contempt for and worked with men, and I liked that," Fisher says. "There was something human about her. It showed that she could do whatever she needed to do, and if she could do that, then everybody could do it. People identified with her. She's like a superhero." (Woerner, "Women")

Nonetheless, she's the goal of the story for Luke – the princess needing rescue, not the hero growing in power. Of course, her most problematic moment is watching her lie there on display in her gold bikini to please Jabba and the male audience. (In Leia's prequel book to *The Force Awakens*, she refuses "a two-piece brown swimsuit adorned with gold braid" and insists on dressing more modestly in a joking homage) (Castellucci 132). Her romance is less problematic, conducted between fellow fighters basically equal in power (most of the time she outranks Han but they're on his ship and neither intimidates the other).

Meanwhile, she values her fighting ability and perception but uses neither to become a Jedi knight. J.J. Abrams notes that he, co-writer Lawrence Kasdan and even George Lucas had discussed this issue together but decided against it:

> It was a great question, and one we talked about quite a bit even with Carrie [Fisher]. If there is 'another' why not

take advantage of this natural Force strength this character had? And one of the answers was that it was simply a choice she made, that her decision to run the rebellion and ultimately this Resistance, and consider herself a General as opposed to a Jedi, it was simply a choice that she took. Not that there isn't any regret that should could have and didn't. But clearly we've seen and we do again, she is clearly Force strong. (Abrams, "Why Didn't")

In the new story, she leads the Resistance, but only behind the scenes.

Like Leia, Padmé starts strong but then fades away, literally. On Tatooine she proves able to explore the desert world and take care of herself, though she only makes feeble protests at Qui-Gon's high-handedness. Episode two, the queen fights for her life in a gladiator pit, but also has her clothing artistically slashed through the revealing white fabric. A great deal of time is spent lounging in gorgeous, impractical outfits while Anakin protects her from scary killers. The third is the worst:

Amidala gives up everything, including the will to live, when the love of her life (Anakin Skywalker) turns to evil. She physically dies of a broken heart while cry-birthing Luke and Leia Skywalker. Padmé doesn't even get the glory of living on as a political martyr; her whole story is swept under the rug so Darth Vader can take the stage. (Woerner, "Women")

All this is why Rey is such a shakeup. Obviously, she's completely strong and capable in every scene. In fact, *Star Wars* not only makes big strides at putting a female front and center, but also at not dwelling on it. No one calls her "princess" or implies she's too sheltered – which she isn't. In fact, she's the first female character growing up outside of privilege – scavenger rather than ruler or senator. "She feels very modern," Lucasfilm President Kathleen Kennedy says of Rey. "I think she will be relevant to audiences today, she embodies that sense of self-reliance and independence. I think that's who she is" (Woerner, "Women").

> Yet it isn't until she meets Finn (John Boyega) where we get to relish watching her defy gender stereotypes. Within minutes of screen time, she disarms Finn with her spear, hides them both from stormtroopers, rescues him — no more hand-holding! — and flies the *Millennium Falcon*. Just like that, Finn is forced to abandon those quaint, traditional gender-role ideas that were programmed into him since birth by the dictatorial First Order. (If only Earth could adapt as quickly.) (Sperling)

On their first meeting, Finn strides in to rescue her, only to see her outfight all the goons attacking her without any help. Working on the Falcon, Finn is helpless with tools and Rey must direct him in another gender-flip. When he infiltrates the Starkiller Base to rescue her, he finds she's already saved herself. Likewise, when he takes on Ren with a lightsaber, Rey is the one to win the duel, then save Finn after. The only one Finn actually rescues is the male Poe.

> "I hope Rey will be something of a girl power figure," Ridley says proudly. "She will have some impact in a girl power-y way. She's brave and she's vulnerable and she's so nuanced ... She doesn't have to be one thing to embody a woman in a film. It just so happens she's a woman but she transcends gender. She's going to speak to men and women." (Howard)

There are other flips on traditional gender roles. Though it's kept family friendly, Kylo Ren violates Rey's mind, and she fights back, violating his in response and reclaiming her power. She reveals him as a scared little boy playing Vader-dress-up rather than a real supervillain.

Rey thus stands out as a shining role model. One critic relates:

> Leaving the theater, my girls felt as empowered as their brother usually does after seeing one of the many blockbusters built for him. They never commented on how pretty Rey is. They never had to flinch because Rey was a sexual object to some man in power. They just felt strong.

79

> Equal. I can only imagine how the film will feel to girls in
> parts of the world where women are not allowed control
> over their own bodies or hearts or minds. Imagine a
> generation of both sexes, growing up believing that girls are
> powerful. Imagine the force of a billion girls realizing that,
> one day, they can rule the galaxy. (Sperling)

Another noticeable change is how the women suddenly
appear everywhere. Maz and Leia ensure that Rey isn't the
only woman in the galaxy – a problem Leia always had.

> The rest of the women in the *Star Wars* prequels and
> originals were sidelined to cantina bar stools or Coruscant
> hallways, banished as background players or imprisoned
> dancers, with the occasional exception of a Mon Mothma
> cameo ("Many Bothans died…"). This list becomes only
> more frustrating when compiled with deleted scenes from
> *Return of the Jedi* that revealed footage of multiple female
> rebel pilots attacking the Death Star. Sadly, most of the lady
> rebels wound up on the cutting-room floor, save for one
> pilot whose small line was dubbed over with the voice of a
> man in the finished film. (Woerner, "Women")

This time, "Abrams acknowledges the past while
fashioning his own pluralistic future filled with a female hero,
female generals, and even Captain Phasma (Gwendoline
Christie), the galaxy's first female villain," added Marlow
Stern in *The Daily Beast*. She concludes: "In this *Star Wars*, the
Force that awakens is woman" (Howard). On Jakku, the first
villager who pulls out a blaster to defend them all from
Stormtroopers is a woman. Female faces casually appear with
Jess the fighter pilot, Rebellion Doctor Kalonia, and some of
the aliens on Jakku and Maz's bar. There's K-T, the pink
companion for R2-D2. Even Leia's biographer droid Peazy
has a female voice. Niima Base itself is named for "old Niima
the Hutt herself" (Fry, *Rey's Survival Guide*). Carrie Fisher
jokes, "It's good to have a little help. I liked being the only
one when I was 19…now I need some backup" (Breznican,
"The Force Awakens" 84).

The Bechdel test (named for comic strip creator Alison

Bechdel) insists that a film or show must meet the following criteria:

1. It includes at least two women
2. who have at least one conversation
3. about something other than a man or men

This is not the only criteria for a feminist film, and it certainly has its flaws as a theory, yet it also emphasizes how many women in films take the role of sidekick or girlfriend whose only purpose is to aid the hero on his quest and worry about his problems. Famously, the first trilogy, with only Leia beside a few shots of Aunt Beru and Mon Mothma, does not pass, despite Leia's strength.

The prequels, however, do, at least somewhat. Episode I has Padmé and Anakin's mother, Shmi, discussing politics. Episode II watches Padmé and the queen discuss whether the Naboo people should leave the Republic. Episode III, however, does not pass, thanks to a lack of conversation between female characters.

More problematic is these heroines' purpose in the stories: Leia is the inspiration for Luke and Han's heroism as they fight to save the princess. Padmé, likewise, is the great catalyst of Anakin's life, fueling his descent into evil. The women's own desires are sublimated under the heroes' struggles and the become only the Anima, the woman who guides the hero to understand his undeveloped feminine side.

Rey, meanwhile, makes her own choices and drives her own narrative. Han, Chewie, and BB-8 appear more to aid her story than their own. While Rey barely encounters Leia onscreen, Maz fills the role of mentor and aids her through the Bechdel issue.

> "*Star Wars* was always a boy's thing, and a movie that dads could take their sons to. And although that is still very much the case, I was really hoping this could be a movie that mothers could take their daughters to as well," Abrams said during a November appearance on "Good Morning America." (Howard)

Maz and Older Leia's roles certainly wave to the mothers as well as daughters. While Yoda is a power fighter in *Attack of the Clones,* Maz's strength seems to derive from quietly surviving, observing, and advising, seeing much that others do not. She's a grandmotherly figure in homespun, unusual in the galaxy and certainly unique to action films.

Maz is in many ways the new queen of the franchise: The symbols on the flags outside her castle include Boba Fett's Mythosaur skull, Ziro the Hutt's Black Sun tattoo, the Broken Horn from *Star Wars: Rebels,* pod racer insignia, and Hondo Ohnaka's pirate symbol. There's also the 501st Legion, international fan-based organization that builds and cosplays armor from the franchise. This subtly suggests that women, even grandmothers, can be fans too – this isn't just a world for teen boys.

There's also the return of Leia, no longer an action girl and young romantic heroine as she used to be, but a loving mother and wife (or at least conflicted ex-wife). Though she's not a nineteen-year-old action heroine, she still gets moments of romance:

> Leia: You know, as much as we fought, I always hated it when you left.
> Han Solo: That's why I did it, so that you'd miss me.
> Leia: I do miss you.

In the novelization, she's shown making more important choices, from sending a representative to plead with the Senate to determining her son's future:

> "[Snoke] knew our child would be strong with the Force. That he was born with equal potential for good or evil."
> "You knew this from the beginning? Why didn't you tell me?"
> She sighed. "Many reasons. I was hoping that I was wrong, that it wasn't true. I hoped I could sway him, turn him away from the dark side, without having to involve you." A small smile appeared. "You had— you have— wonderful

qualities, Han, but patience and understanding were never among them. I was afraid that your reactions would only drive him farther to the dark side. I thought I could shield him from Snoke's influence and you from what was happening."
Her voice dropped. "It's clear now that I was wrong. Whether your involvement would have made a difference, we'll never know."

Along with her relationship with her rebellious son (described but not seen onscreen) she takes a motherly interest in Rey, the new romantic and action heroine. Of course, Rey is likely either her daughter or her niece – many viewers wondered if before Leia's embrace and farewell, Leia imparted this information. She sends Rey off with "May the Force be with you," symbolically passing the torch of adventuring to the next generation. As the mature princess and love interest, she's another character unusual in this sort of film.

Another twist is that Phasma, the "Chrome Trooper" played by Gwendoline Christie, was originally designed as male.

After *The Force Awakens* unveiled its first cast photo, featuring only one new female character, online media outlets (including *io9*) criticized the male-dominated cast— and it turns out this was a major factor in their decision.
"Everything was happening simultaneously," [writer Lawrence] Kasdan told *Vulture*. "When the idea came up to make Phasma female, it was instantaneous: Everyone just said, 'Yes. That's great.'" (Lussier, "Gwendoline Christie")

While this Stormtrooper captain role would generally be taken by a man, the more interesting fact is that she never removes her mask – only her long ponytail and voice identify her as female.

"What feels so modern about Captain Phasma is that we are used to forming our immediate relationships with female characters, conventionally, due to the way they are made flesh," Christie told *io9*. "So for us to form our immediately and initial relationship with this character, who happens to be a female character, who happens to be *Star Wars'* first female villain on screen, I felt that was really modern. That we respond to her through her character and her actions initially rather than the way she's made flesh." (Lussier, "Gwendoline Christie")

Her appearance emphasizes that the Empire and its splinter groups have women (and perhaps have always had women no one has seen) Likewise, the First Order has seemingly shed the speciesist philosophies of the old Empire, since now their leader Snoke is an alien. In a universe where aliens represent people of color, this is a clear shift in the metaphor. No longer are the Aryan Nazis preying on the Wookies and other marginalized races.

More directly, people of color are now scattered through the universe, along with women. Casually in many scenes, there are more Blacks and Asians among the Resistance or in the gangs that board Han Solo's ship. Leia's second-in-command is the Asian Admiral Statura. With Poe (whose actor, Oscar Isaac, is Guatemalan), and Finn (John Boyega) front and center, the universe has a lots more diversity all of a sudden. Finn's unmasking in fact suggests the Stormtroopers might be any race now, unlike their sameness in *Attack of the Clones*. Thus the universe is being rewritten in a way that allows fans of all races and genders to join in the fun.

Of course, there are still barriers to fight past onscreen. Helen O'Hara, provocative author of "*Star Wars* Hero Poe Dameron: Is Disney Brave Enough to Make him Gay?" writes: "The time would seem to be coming where we could and should have a hotshot X-wing pilot who happens to be gay." She adds:

When reunited after believing one another dead, Poe runs towards Finn and throws himself into an embrace; if Finn were a woman, we'd be in little doubt that that was enough to signal interest. Should we doubt it just because they're both men? *The Force Awakens* radically put a woman and a black man front-and-centre; why not add a gay man and complete a trifecta of the underrepresented?

Certainly, Poe and Finn are close, and Poe isn't seen caring for Rey or any other woman onscreen or in his books. The actors played with the issue in an interview while leaving everything open:

> "I think it's very subtle romance that's happening; you have to watch it a few times to see the little hints. At least I was playing romance; in the cockpit I was playing romance," joked Oscar Isaac on Ellen the day before the movie came out.
>
> Boyega agreed, "I was playing romance," – though it wasn't clear that he was talking about the same scene, or that he was any more serious.
>
> Isaac finished by saying, "I won't say with which character. It could be a droid." (O'Hara)

A REY OF HOPE

REY AS MARY SUE

Is Rey too powerful? The term "Mary Sue" is floating around the internet. A Mary Sue is a wish fulfillment character, generally representing the author. She can outdo the main characters at all the things they're best at and easily rescues them. They adore her for it, instantly and completely. She also displays total flawlessness, except perhaps for a quirk everyone finds "cute."

Rey exudes many traces of this as she enters the *Star Wars* world and gets to steal the Millennium Falcon, fight in space battles, have an astromech droid sidekick. Leia embraces her and blesses her. She receives Luke Skywalker's lightsaber (in fact, it chooses her!) and goes questing to find him and be his student.

But all this fandom fun isn't the big problem – it's her skillset.

While she's a talented fighter, she's never used a lightsaber before her great battle with Kylo Ren – who's trained with Luke himself from childhood as well as the Super Sith Lord Snoke. Nonetheless, she beats him, using a blend of reaching for the serenity within and acting with apparent rage and exertion in a less likely display of power. Yoda already told us the Dark Side isn't *more* powerful.

At the helm of the Millennium Falcon, a vessel which always has a co-pilot, she flies it well enough not only to escape several TIE fighters, but to point the ship so Finn can shoot the last one out of the sky with a broken gun. Growing up on the desert planet, she's scavenged ships and flown a speeder, but the first movie emphasizes that a desert farm kid with a speeder is far different from a pilot who can manage the big ship in deep space and evade Stormtroopers. The prequel books add that she played on simulators as well, but that doesn't seem like enough.

She speaks every language, having taught herself this along with repairs, flying, staff fighting, and salvaging. This is a long list of skills, all the more impressive because she was left on her own (as far as the story vaguely suggests) at age *six* or so on a hostile desert planet.

In the book she also offers a crucial suggestion, much like Luke's proposal of shooting the exhaust ports:

> "I've seen inside these kinds of walls," she told them as the sky overhead continued to rain destruction. "The mechanics and instrumentation are the same as the Star Destroyers I've spent years inside salvaging. Get me to a conventional junction station, I can get us in."

Even her heedless decisions like running off into the forest and protecting BB-8 from her boss have no serious repercussions – she fights off everyone who comes after her. She's never injured, unlike Poe after his own torture session. When Kylo Ren invades her mind, she invades his back while still barely knowing what the Force is. Likewise, in a moment that seems more fan-fun than realism, she controls the Stormtrooper guard and makes him release her.

She's better than Han at fixing the Milennium Falcon and Han and Chewie, like Finn, instantly adore her. She's too skilled in too many areas.

Of course, is this terrible? One critic notes:

> The kids who make up much of *Star Wars'* audience can use a self-insertion figure, someone they can easily imagine being if they were plopped into this universe. *Force Awakens* has just made that figure a woman, instead of a man, and Rey is instantly the most compelling new character in the film. (VanDerWerff)

Critic Tasha Robinson adds that Rey is "a fantasy wish-fulfillment character with outsized skills, an inhuman reaction time, and a clever answer to every question — but so are the other major *Star Wars* heroes" (Howard).

Of course, Luke is likeable and he's nowhere near as talented. He makes a lucky shot or too with help from the Force but is far from a weapons expert. Luke can't hypnotize people until his third film, with deliberate training from two Jedi Masters. He loses his lightsaber battle at Bespin against a better-trained foe. He never learns to read minds. His growth and change, as well as terrible defeat in *Empire Strikes Back* teach him as a person. Rey gets none of this herself.

"The fight for equal representation for women, in front of and behind the camera, continues, and will continue for a long time. No one's saying sexism is over and we should put our feet up and enjoy it. And no one's arguing that all female characters should be as flawless and fearless as Rey," wrote Tasha Robinson for *The Verge*. "Characters who have a lot to overcome to become heroes are the bravest and most inspirational — more so than characters like Rey, who are naturally good at everything." (Howard)

WORKS CITED

Primary Sources

Aaron, Jason and John Cassaday. *Star Wars 6: Skywalker Strikes, Part VI*. New York: Marvel, 3 June 2015.

Aaron, Jason and Stuart Immonen. *Star Wars 8: Showdown on the Smuggler's Moon Part I*. New York: Marvel, 19 Aug 2015.

—. *Star Wars 11: Showdown on the Smuggler's Moon Part IV*. New York: Marvel, 4 Nov 2015.

—. *Star Wars 12: Showdown on the Smuggler's Moon Part V*. New York: Marvel, 18 Nov 2015.

Castellucci, Cecil. *Moving Target: A Princess Leia Adventure*. USA: Disney Lucasfilm Press, 2015.

Dawson, Delilah S. *The Perfect Weapon (Star Wars)*. USA: Disney Lucasfilm Press, 2015.

Foster, Alan Dean. *Star Wars: The Force Awakens*. USA: LucasBooks, 2-15. Kindle Edition.

Fry, Jason. *Rey's Survival Guide*. USA: Readers Digest, 2015.

—. *The Weapon of a Jedi: A Luke Skywalker Adventure*. USA: Disney Lucasfilm Press, 2015.

Gray, Claudia and Phil Noto. *Lost Stars*. USA: Disney Lucasfilm Press, 2015.

Noto, Phil. *Star Wars: Before the Awakening (Digital Picture Book)*. USA: Disney Lucasfilm Press, 2015.

Rucka, Greg and Marco Chechetto. *Shattered Empire*. New York: Marvel, 2015.

Rucka, Greg. *Smuggler's Run: A Han Solo Adventure*. USA: Disney Lucasfilm Press, 2015.

Walker, Landry Q. *All Creatures Great and Small: Tales From a*

Galaxy Far, Far Away. USA: Disney Lucasfilm Press, 2015.

—. *The Crimson Corsair and the Lost Treasure of Count Dooku: Tales From a Galaxy Far, Far Away.* USA: Disney Lucasfilm Press, 2015.

—. *The Face of Evil: Tales From a Galaxy Far, Far Away.* USA: Disney Lucasfilm Press, 2015.

—. *High Noon on Jakku: Tales From a Galaxy Far, Far Away.* USA: Disney Lucasfilm Press, 2015.

Wallace, Daniel and Annie Stoll. *Star Wars Rebels: Sabine My Rebel Sketchbook.* USA: Reader's Digest, 2015.

Wendig, Chuck. *Aftermath.* USA: Disney Lucasfilm Press, 2015.

Secondary Sources

Abrams, J.J."Why Leia Didn't Become a Jedi." *IGN,* 7 Dec 2015. Online video
http://www.ign.com/videos/2015/12/07/star-wars-the-force-awakens-why-leia-didnt-become-a-jedi

Anders, Charlie Jane. *"Star Wars: The Force Awakens* Is the Most Fun I've Had at the Movies in Ages." *IO9,* 16 Dec 2015. http://io9.gizmodo.com/star-wars-the-force-awakens-is-the-most-fun-ive-had-at-1748271186

Anderton, Ethan. "Ewan McGregor, Alec Guiness and Frank Oz Are All in *Star Wars: The Force Awakens.*" *SlashFilm,* 20 Dec 2015. http://www.slashfilm.com/you-can-hear-alec-guinness-and-ewan-mcgregor-in-the-force-awakens

Baker-Whitelaw, Gavia. *"Star Wars: The Force Awakens* gives us another beautiful three-way friendship.*Daily Dot,* 21 Dec 2015. http://www.dailydot.com/geek/star-wars-force-awakens-finn-rey-poe-ot3-friendship-romance/

Barr, Tricia. "Luke Skywalker's Journey to Heroism." *Star Wars Insider 2016 Special Edition* 2015. 6-11.

"BB-8." *People Special Star Wars: The Force Awakens Edition,* Dec 2015. 63.

"Billie Lourd." *People Special Star Wars: The Force Awakens*

Edition, Dec 2015. 52.

Breznican, Anthony. "The First Order" *Entertainment Weekly: The Ultimate Guide to Star Wars,* 2015. 90-91.

—. "The Force Awakens." *Entertainment Weekly: The Ultimate Guide to Star Wars,* 2015. 78-85.

—."*Star Wars: The Force Awakens:* J.J. Abrams Reveals Backstory of Alien Maz Kanata." *Entertainment Weekly,* 11 Dec 2015.
http://www.ew.com/article/2015/11/12/star-wars-force-awakens-lupita-nyongo-maz-kanata

Bruce-Mitford, Miranda. *The Illustrated Book of Signs and Symbols.* USA: DK Publishing, 1996.

Campbell, Joseph. *The Hero with a Thousand Faces.* New York: Princeton University Press, 1973.

--. *Pathways to Bliss: Mythology and Personal Transformation.* Novato, CA: New World Library, 2004.

Campbell, Joseph with Bill Moyers, *The Power of Myth,* ed. Betty Sue Flowers, New York: Doubleday, 1988.

Canavan, Gerry. "From "A New Hope" to no Hope at All: "Star Wars," Tolkien and the Sinister and Depressing Reality of Expanded Universes." *Salon* 24 Dec 2015.
http://www.salon.com/2015/12/24/from_a_new_hope_to_no_hope_at_all_star_wars_tolkien_and_the_sinister_and_depressing_reality_of_expanded_universes/

Castellucci, Cecil "Writers on Writing: Claudia Gray and Cecil Castellucci." *StarWars.com,* 11 Dec 2015.
http://www.starwars.com/news/writers-on-writing-claudia-gray-and-cecil-castellucci

Cirlot, J.E. *A Dictionary of Symbols.* New York: Routledge, 1971.

Cox, Carolyn. "Whiny Babies Complain About LGBTQ+ Characters in *Star Wars,* Chuck Wendig Responds Excellently." *The Mary Sue,* 8 Sept 2015.
http://www.themarysue.com/naboo-hoo-hoo.

"Director J.J. Abrams." *People Special Star Wars: The Force Awakens Edition,* Dec 2015. 66.

Dodgens, Wes. "The Corruption of Powerful Symbols." *Star*

Wars in the Classroom. EDventure Quest Learning LLC. 2012. http://www.starwarsintheclassroom.com/content/ss/history/corrupting_symbols.asp

Frankel, Valerie Estelle. *Buffy and the Heroine's Journey*. USA: McFarland and Co., 2012.

—. *From Girl to Goddess*. USA: McFarland and Co., 2010.

—. *The Many Faces of Katniss Everdeen: Exploring the Heroine of The Hunger Games*. USA: Winged Lion Press, 2013.

Fry, Jason and Kemp Remillard. *Star Wars: The Force Awakens Incredible Cross-Sections*. USA: Disney Lucasfilm Press, 2015.

Hidalgo, Pablo. *Star Wars: The Force Awakens Visual Dictionary*. USA: Disney Lucasfilm Press, 2015.

Howard, Adam. "*Star Wars: The Force Awakens* Hero Rey Hailed as Feminist Icon." *MSNBC*, 22 Dec 2015. http://www.msnbc.com/msnbc/star-wars-the-force-awakens-hero-rey-hailed-feminist-icon.

Keyes, Rob. "Luke Skywalker's Role in *Star Wars: The Force Awakens* Explained." *ScreenRant* 20 Dec 2015. http://screenrant.com/star-wars-7-luke-skywalker-role-explained/

Lussier, Germain. "Gwendoline Christie Didn't Know that Captain Phasma Was Originally a Man." *IO9*, 7 Dec 2015. http://io9.gizmodo.com/gwendoline-christie-didnt-know-that-captain-phasma-was-1746696902

Moran, Sarah. "*Star Wars:* How Rey Brings Balance to the Franchise." *SlashFilm*, 21 Dec 2015. http://screenrant.com/star-wars-force-awakens-rey-female-characters/comment-page-1/#comments

Mounet Lipp, Gerhard and Bambi. "ML Mural Art." *Family Trees and Crests*. http://www.familytreesandcrests.com/heraldry-symbols.htm

O'Hara, Helen. "Star Wars Hero Poe Dameron: Is Disney Brave Enough to Make him Gay?" *Telegraph* 1 Jan 2016. http://www.telegraph.co.uk/film/star-wars-the-force-awakens/poe-dameron-gay-disney.

"Queen of the Desert." *People Special Star Wars: The Force Awakens Edition,* Dec 2015. 74.

"Returning Cinema's Greatest Space Saga to the Screen." *Entertainment Weekly: The Ultimate Guide to Star Wars,* 2015. 86-87.

Robinson, Joanna. "A Rey of Light." *Vanity Fair,* 16 Dec 2015. http://www.vanityfair.com/hollywood/2015/12/star-wars-force-awakens-daisy-ridley-rey-feminist-bechdel-test

Shepherd, Rowena and Rupert. *1000 Symbols.* New York: The Ivy Press, 2002.

Sperling, Nicole. "The Power of Rey: Daisy Ridley's *Star Wars* Heroine is an Instant Icon." *Entertainment Weekly,* 12 Dec 2015. http://www.ew.com/article/2015/12/22/star-wars-force-awakens-rey

Star Wars Database http://www.starwars.com

Szostak, Phil. *The Art of Star Wars: The Force Awakens.* USA: Abrams Books, 2015.

Ultimate Sticker Collection: Star Wars: The Force Awakens. USA: DK Children, 2015.

VanDerWerff, Todd. *"Star Wars: The Force Awakens:* 5 Ways the New Movie Copies the Original Film." *Vox,* 21 Dec. 2015. http://www.vox.com/2015/12/21/10632690/star-wars-the-force-awakens-spoilers-han-solo-new-hope

Vogler, Christopher. *The Writer's Journey.* USA: Michael Wiese Productions, 1998.

Von Franz, Marie Louise. *The Feminine in Fairy Tales.* USA: Shambhala 1993.

—. "The Process of Individuation." *Man and his Symbols.* Ed. Carl G. Jung. New York: Doubleday and Co., 1964. 158-229.

Walker, Barbara G. *The Woman's Dictionary of Symbols and Sacred Objects.* San Francisco: Harper, 1988.

Woerner, Meredith. "Adam Driver of *Star Wars* Reflects on the Man behind the Mask, Kylo Ren." *LA Times* 21 Dec

2015.
http://www.latimes.com/entertainment/herocomplex/la
-et-hc-star-wars-adam-driver-20151221-story.html

—."The Women of *Star Wars* Speak out about their New
Empire." *LA Times,* 4 Dec 2015.
http://www.latimes.com/entertainment/herocomplex/la
-ca-hc-the-women-of-star-wars-the-force-awakens-
20151206-htmlstory.html

Zweig, Connie. "The Conscious Feminine: Birth of a New
Archetype," *Mirrors of the Self: Archetypal Images that Shape
Your Life.* Ed. Christine Downing. New York: St. Martin's
Press, 1991. 183-191.

ABOUT THE AUTHOR

Valerie Estelle Frankel is the author of many books on pop culture, including *Doctor Who – The What, Where, and How*, *Sherlock: Every Canon Reference You May Have Missed in BBC's Series 1-3*, *History, Homages and the Highlands: An Outlander Guide*, and *How Game of Thrones Will End*. Many of her books focus on women's roles in fiction, from her heroine's journey guides *From Girl to Goddess* and *Buffy and the Heroine's Journey* to books like *Women in Game of Thrones* and *The Many Faces of Katniss Everdeen*. Once a lecturer at San Jose State University, she's a frequent speaker at conferences. Come explore her research at www.vefrankel.com.

www.ingramcontent.com/pod-product-compliance
Lightning Source LLC
Chambersburg PA
CBHW020512030426
42337CB00011B/357